The Floral
Charm
of Cyprus

*including Shrubs, Trees
and Wild Life*

by
VALERIE SINCLAIR

INTERWORLD
PUBLICATIONS

Interworld Publications
(Tophill Advertising & Promotions Ltd)
12 The Fairway, New Barnet
Hertfordshire, EN5 1HN, England
Fax: 081-447 0599

First published in 1992

ISBN: 0 948853 16 6

Typeset in Century Schoolbook by
  Sunset Typesetters
Designed and planned by Tophill Designs
Colour Separations by Lee Terry
Printed and bound in Cyprus by
  PRINTCO LTD.

Contents

A Floral Carpet

A thousand years before the clumsy feet of mortal man
This island's flowers flourished in the reign of mighty Pan,
When Aphrodite's hand-maidens took over Nature's looms
To weave a floral carpet from the multi-coloured blooms.

Man-made mosaics of later date and beautiful, but still
Do not compare for colour with this rainbow's overspill;
Pink Cyclamen, blue lavender, white narcissus entice
Our careful feet to wander through this earthly paradise.

Now we inherit these delights: in our protection lies
The future of these miracles and in our children's eyes
If we can show we understand environmental fears
Then Cyprus will stay blooming for another thousand years.

INTRODUCTION
by
Phryne Michael

It has given me a great pleasure to accept, on behalf of the Cyprus Tourism Organisation, the request of Ms Valerie Sinclair to introduce her lovely publication **'The Floral Charm of Cyprus'**.

I am confident that this publication, which is dedicated to the floral richness of Cyprus will serve as a nature guide for those who wish to get acquainted with the floral world of the island.

The flora of Cyprus is unique and diversified with a vast variety of flowering plants, of which some are endemic, occuring nowhere else in the world but in Cyprus, and a great variety of habitats ranging from desert to alpine.

Not only scientists but also amateur observers have been expressing a great interest in getting to know the island's floral variety, which decorates nearly every season of the year in a very special way, and co-exists harmoniously with the ancient monuments which are scattered around the island.

The natural beauty of Cyprus is a wealth that we all should take care of and treasure and every attempt towards this direction has definitely the support of Cyprus Tourism Organisation.

Publications like the present one, contribute also in making us all more conscious about the environment, the conservation of which has become a matter of vital importance.

Phryne Michael
Director-General
Cyprus Tourism Organisation

Dedicated to my dear husband Ian

A Floral Path Through Cyprus

A seasonal selection of some of the more interesting and colourful wild flowers which enhance the natural charm of Cyprus.

This small guide will hopefully become a companion for flower lovers who like myself love to roam this beautiful island, discovering some of the rarer plants which enrich and carpet the countryside. There is so much enjoyment to be gained from the sight and scent of popular flowers encountered each year, and the discovery of a particular wild flower for the first time can be most exciting. Furthermore searching for flowers in the hills and mountains can add another dimension to walking and climbing.

Mountain flowers are often small and delicate, tucked away in sheltered crannies in the rocks or peeping out from ledges and other crevices.

During the Spring, fields and hillsides that may otherwise go unnoticed sparkle with intense and vibrant colour, covered in a wild profusion of delicate blooms. A feeling of optimism pervades the air "Summer is on its way". The gentle Mediterranean sun is coaxing the land into life.

To someone from a less sunny clime a brilliant yellow carpet of crown daisies interspersed with bright red poppies and anemones can dazzle the eye; similarly the tiny rich purple flowers of the **Romulea** as they rest like little cushions on the surfaces of rocks. Despite their small size close examination, preferably with a magnifying glass, reveals tiny delicate patterns. The anemones also show subtle variations in colour and structure. In December the white variety can be seen on the plains extending later to the hills, followed by red, pink, pale lavender, violet and purple, blooming profusely until April.

The varied climate in Cyprus together with its diverse topography contribute to a very colourful and interesting flora. The flowering season differs from the lowlands to the highlands where plants are seen growing to various heights.

Flowers bloom in a wonderful profusion of colours during March and April. In May and June the annuals die and many shed their seeds. During the summer, when the ground becomes parched and dry, many plants cease to grow but, below the ground, the perennials survive in the form of bulbs, tubers or corms which multiply in readiness for the new season in the Autumn.

For visitors to Cyprus during the summer months, it is however still possible to find flowers in bloom if you know where to look. For example, there are plants growing close to the sea which are in full bloom even when the ground is so dry and parched. In May a creeper called **Sea Medick** forms a yellow carpet along the sandy shores. It has a very robust root which absorbs water from deep into the ground. From June through to August, the **Sea Holly** becomes prevalent along the beaches. Similar to the **Sea Medick** it has a hardy root for absorbing moisture. It is recognisable by its numerous blue flowers in compact flowering heads and its greyish-blue leaves so prickly to the touch. Take care where you walk.

In August and September it is so pleasant to take an evening stroll along the beach when the air is cooler and filled with the sweet fragrance of the **Sand Lily** *(Krinos tou Gialou* in Greek). This elegant white flower stands out so proudly against the dark yellow sand. Unfortunately careless people in the past have caused its numbers to decline. Please remember to treat it with respect so others can enjoy this wondrous specimen.

If you take your car up into the mountains, a number of plants many of which are endemic to Cyprus, can be seen, adding a welcome splash of colour to the bare grey rocks. For example *Alyssum troodi* sits in the crannies of rocks forming brilliant yellow cushions throughout the whole of May and June. In June and July, another splash of yellow will dazzle you as you approach the Chionistra slopes, a small shrub called **Prickly Broom** *(Raski* in Greek).

I have compiled the plants as I have observed them coming into season starting with October. I have shown each plant's Latin name, the family to which it belongs, its English name and its Greek translation. The Latin names used are at the time of writing those shown in R.D. Meikle's book "Flora of Cyprus". The English names for Mediterranean plants are not always completely accurate and are based on common usage. The Greek names are those used most often by the villagers and sometimes vary from district to district. Very often they are quite different from those used in Greece.

I have attempted to illustrate most of the flowers portrayed in a simple but colourful way which I trust will nevertheless help you to identify them. The watercolours were painted by myself but I would like to thank the following friends for contributing the lovely photographs:-

Mr. Renos Lavithis

Mrs. Mary Guth

Mr. John Taylor

Mr. Yiannis Christofides of the Minerva Hotel, Platres

Mr. Pambos Christodolou from the Forestry Dept.
of the Ministry of Agriculture.

Mr. Takis Papacristoforo from the Forestry Dept.
of the Ministry of Agriculture.

Mr. Apostolos Potamos of FOTO CARE, Paphos

George Wiedl Hans-Jorg's

I would also like to thank Anna and Renos Lavithis, the publishers, for all their help and advice. Also, a big thank you to my husband, not only for his constant support, but also for the delightful little poems he composed which enhance some of the illustrations.

As it was the medicinal properties of plants which first prompted their study, I have devoted a chapter to this subject and thought it appropriate to mention any herbal or medicinal qualities any particular plant may have. I feel this might be of interest to some if not all of my readers.

Many of these plants are used by the islands in their cuisine and so for those of you interested in Mediterranean cookery, a few paragraphs have been devoted to their culinary properties. For further reading on this subject, I would suggest a delightful little book called "A Taste of Cyprus" written by Gilli Davies, which gives a seasonal look at Cypriot cookery.

The study of flowers is an absorbing and rewarding hobby. It need not involve strenuous activity — just a little time and an appreciation of natural beauty. My book is not intended to be a technical one, just a simple guide to help you with identification. For those of you who would like more detailed descriptions of the plants in a botanical way, I would suggest the following reading material:—

Flora of Cyprus (2 vols) by R.D. Meikle Kew

Flowers of the Mediterranean by Oleg Polunin and Anthony Huxley

Flowers of Cyprus (Plants of Medicine) by Chr. Georgiades (2 vols) Nicosia.

Wild Flowers of Cyprus Reputed to have Medicinal Qualities

Plants have always played a vital role in the history of Cyprus. People living in the rural areas use a large number of wild flowers as food, perfumes, pot-pourries, medicines and dyes. The geographical location of the island, its varied climate and the different types of soil result in a wealth of plant life.

A treatise on Euphorbiacea, written by King Juba of Mauretania, some 2000 years ago, detailed its great value as a purgative. The plant which is called *"Euphorbia helioscopia* (**Sun Spurge**) was named by the King after his physician Euphorbisis.

During the 1st Century AD Pedanius Dioscorides wrote his treatise called "De Materia Medica", which dealt with the properties of 600 plants. About the same time, a Roman Civil Servant called Gaius, Plinius Secundus, or Pliny the Elder, wrote "Historia Naturalis", which included several books on medical botany. The volume of this work made it a valuable source of reference.

Of course, there were others who wrote extensively on this subject in former times, writers such as Hippocrates, born 460 BC, and Theophrastus, born 370 BC. The renowned works of Hippocrates, a famous Greek doctor, included about 400 simple herbal remedies, stressing the importance of diet and hygiene. This concept was developed later by Galen, another Greek physician, in the 2nd Century AD.

"The Enquiry of Plants" written by Theophrastus a century after Hippocrates, concentrated mainly on the structure of plants and he was the first writer to classify them.

Carl von Linné, a Swedish professor of Botany, more usually known as Linnaeus, revolutionised the whole method of naming and classifying plants which was subsequently improved upon. To avoid confusion, he gave plants Latin or scientific names based upon two words e.g. *Convolvolus arvensis*. The first or generic name has a capital letter, and this indicates how the plant is classified, followed by the specific name of the individual species which shows what makes the plant different from others e.g. *"arvensis"* means "of the field". These names are constantly being up-dated by a group of eminent Botanists who form the International Nomenclature Committee.

Following the great classical works, physicians during the Middle Ages used many herbs in medicine. Paracelsus, an Italian doctor, (1493-1541), also made a study of plants and introduced many mineral drugs. He is quoted as saying that "landscapes and hills are indeed true pharmacies".

At about the same time, an Act of Parliament was passed in England proclaiming that anyone having a knowledge of the healing properties of plants was allowed to make use of such knowledge. This was claimed as a charter by many practitioners of folk medicine and they became known as herbalists. At the beginning of this century, very few herbs were recognised as being of any use by the medical profession. Today, however, about 40% of the world's drugs are of plant origin, plants which centuries ago had been used in folk medicine. Nowadays, our society is tired of reading about the side effects attached to chemical drugs and is showing a marked interest in the more natural cures from plant life.

This renewed interest we hope will not only benefit mankind but also contribute to the protection and conservation of plants in general.

The use of plants in medicine is often associated with magic and superstition. Many such plants were protected by mere legend and myth. The Ancient Greeks, for example considered that **"Violets"** were the symbol of virginity and the flowers were used to adorn the nuptial bed. There is a legend which decrees that violets are a symbol of Adam's tears after he was banished from the Garden of Eden. In medicine both the flowers and tubers have since been used to treat coughs and respiratory infections. Another example, **"St. John's Wort,"** very prolific on the island, was said to protect humans, animals and buildings against demons and evil spirits, and on St. John's Eve, the 23rd June, the plants were passed through smoke to make them even more powerful.

Another plant steeped in legend, the **"paeony"** which was brought to Cyprus by medieval monks for its medicinal qualities, was said (by Plato) to have been used by Peon, the Healer of Gods, to treat Plato for certain ailments. The plant has been used extensively since as a pain killer and tranquilliser.

Another legend, referring to the **"Alkanna"** plant, said that if one chews a piece of this plant and then spits it out over a snake, the snake would die. Today **Alkanna** is fried by some villagers as a delicacy and used as a colouring agent in food; also, in cosmetics as a dye.

The plant called **"Mandrake"** must be the one most shrouded in mystery and superstition. In early herbal books, the root is usually represented by a human figure often accompanied by a dog. It was thought that any person digging up the roots of the **"Mandrake"** would instantly be struck dead on hearing it scream. To avert this a dog was tied to the shoot and dog food placed just out of its reach. The dog struggled and eventually pulled up the root, sacrificing its life in the heroic process. The root of **"Mandrake"** was often wrapped in silk and placed in a special box. In Biblical times the plant was thought to induce fertility and this is why the plant is commonly known as **"Love Apple"**. Since early Classical times, the plant has been used as an anaesthetic during operations and later on as a treatment for rheumatism.

In the Middle Ages, it was noted that certain parts of a plant might resemble, in form or colour, some part of the human body. It was believed that diseases of the said organ could be cured by the application of the corresponding plant. For instance, the **"liverwort"** was so named because it resembled a liver in shape. Hence, it was used for liver complaints; the **"lungwort"** (a plant allied to the **Borage** family) whose leaves resemble the lungs was for lung ailments. The **Orchid** is believed to have taken its name from its tubers which resemble the male testes, therefore believed valuable in curing diseases of the male sex organs. Also, the yellow colour of saffron from the stigma of the **"crocus"** was thought to resemble bile and in consequence of this was used in the treatment of biliousness.

The Ancient Greeks used to hang up inside their houses the bulbs called **"Sea Squill"** in order to deter disease. Today the bulbs are used in medicine for heart disease and as a remedy for coughs.

Animals as well as humans are considered to have benefited from plants with herbal qualities. Many years ago the peasants in Cyprus discovered that their sheep and goats stood resistant to snake bites if they were encouraged to eat the plant commonly known as **"Spanish Broom"**. They also gave their donkeys capsules made from the **"Corn Poppy"** for a tonic, and still today prepare eye lotions from this plant to cure eye infections in their animals. For diarrhoea and other intestinal problems, they give their animals **"Wild Mignonette"** in its dried form or the root of the **"Mullein"** plant.

The landscape in Cyprus is rich in herbs and their use in medicine, cosmetics and cooking is extensive. How does one recognise a herb from other plants? The simple answer is that herbs do not have any woody stems above the ground. They die down in winter and pass the season either as a stem underground, or else the whole plant dies and only seeds remain to reproduce the plant. Sometimes the underground stem takes various shapes known as a rhizome, tuber, corm or bulb, to which roots are attached. Examples of the most common herbs grown in Cyprus are, **Sage, Thyme, Common Borage** and **Naples Garlic.**

From historical and archaeological studies we now have extensive lists of plants used by the ancients in the art of healing. We can also learn from modern literature and present day culture which plants are collected and used medicinally. However, I would like to mention here that none of the plants described in this book should be used for healing or curing ailments except under the guidance of a skilled practitioner. Even plants frequently used by the villagers in Cyprus may be dangerous in the wrong doses, or if the wrong part of the plant be taken.

For your interest only I have appended on the next two pages a number of popular wild flowers growing in Cyprus which have been reputed to have medicinal qualities.

Wild Flowers growing on Cyprus which have been reputed to have medicinal qualities are:-

English name	Greek name	
Meadow Saffron	*Krokos*	Rheumatism, gout
Polyanthus Narcissus	*Mitsikorudho*	Pain killer, tranquilliser (Strictly on professional advice)
Jacks Cowl	*Koukkoula*	Gastritis, catarrh, bronchitis and snake bites.
Cyclamen	*Kyklamino*	Rheumatism, arthritis (Strictly on professional advice)
Golden Henbane	*Demonario*	Pain killer, tranquilliser (Strictly on professional advice)
Cape Sorrel	*Oxinudhi*	Dermatitis
Calendula	*Karagiozis*	Wounds and Ulcers
Love Apple	*Kalanthropos*	Anaesthetic, rheumatism
Neopolitan Garlic	*Agroskortho*	Disinfectant, antiseptic
Borage	*Boratsino*	Antiseptic, colds, rheumatism
Tall Asphodel	*Asphodelos*	Diarrhoea
Spiny Burnet	*Mazi*	Tonic, Diuretic
Rock Rose	*Xistari*	Infection
Winged Pea	*Magoutso*	Blood purifier, anti-spasmodic
Iris	*Irida*	Emollient, sedative
Dead Nettle	*Skilakia*	Prostatis, Uterus disorders
Squirting Cucumber	*Pikragurka*	Purgative, rheumatism, shingle
Purple Clover	*Agrio Triphyllas*	Diuretic, sore throats
Leontice	*Voidokratis*	Migraine, epilepsy

English name	Greek name	
Sword Lily	*Macheras*	Sterility
Common Mallow	*Molocha*	Intestinal Disorders, inflammation
Sage	*Spatzia*	Respiratory infections, sore throats
Common Fumitory	*Kapnos*	Laxative, stomach disorders
Myrtle	*Mersini*	Antiseptic, sinisitis, nasal decongestant
Sea Lily	*Krinos tou Yialou*	Emetic
Caper	*Cappari*	Antiseptic, diuretic
Blackberry	*Vatos*	Diarrhoea, ulcers, intestinal infestions

I would like to emphasise that none of the plants I have listed here are recommended by me for the complaints they are reputed to cure. Professional advice should always be taken first.

Wild Flowers of Cyprus with Cosmetic Qualities

From ancient times herbs have been collected and dried for use in cosmetics and perfumery. It is obvious from earlier recordings that the Egyptians and Greeks were preoccupied with making perfumes and bathing in scented waters as well as blending face packs from aromatic herbs. Although it was actually an Arabian doctor called Avicenna in the 10th Century who discovered the secret of distilling essential oils from wild flowers (a process used assiduously since then), the first recorded recipe for cold cream was found to be invented by a Greek physician called Galen as early as the 2nd Century, A.D.

In an increasingly technological age, society is showing a renewed interest in more natural products now it has been discovered that these are less likely to produce allergic reactions than their chemical counterparts.

An enormous variety of wild flowers growing in Cyprus can be used either as the main ingredients for cosmetics or as subtle additives.

There are many advantages for making cosmetics at home apart from the absence of allergic reactions mentioned above. For example, everyone has a different skin-type and the ingredients for emollient creams can thus be varied to suit each person. Similarly, in hair cosmetics, oily skin needs regular cleaning to prevent blocked pores developing into blackheads, hence astringent herbs would be advised e.g. **nettle.**

Dry skin which always feels taught and flakes easily in the hot Cyprus sun, also prone to wrinkling, would require a rich moisturising cream made from **camomile** or **marigold.**

Sensitive skin which sometimes reacts violently to the sun and insect bites, would need a light infusion of **parsley, chervil** or **elderflower** when cleansing.

A simple moisturising lotion can be made from about one ounce of fresh **camomile, meadowsweet** or **elderflowers** soaked in 75ml or one eighth of a pint of warm milk, covered for approximately three hours, strained, reheated and a little honey dissolved in the liquid. A spoonful of oat or wheat bran can be added to thicken the lotion. The mixture should then be bottled and refrigerated and used within a week.

Another very effective lotion to help smooth rough skin, a common problem in Cyprus, can be made from an eighth of a pint (75ml) of **camomile** infusion, added to it, 6 teaspoons of glycerine (available from pharmacies) and cucumber juice made from squeezing 12oz cucumber.

An infusion of astringent herbs to rinse the face after cleansing can be used as a refreshing toner e.g. **dandelion, fennel, rosemary** and **elderflower** especially for oil skin; equal quantities of the infusion

ixed with **rosewater** or **orange-flower** water for dry skins. It should
 noted that fresh herb infusions will not keep longer than a few days.
owdered orris root from the **iris** plant can be used as a preservative.
stringent herbs, scented flower waters, citrus fruits, spices and herb
inegars are all well-known ingredients for making skin lotions and
nics.

A simple way to make bath-water scented is to make a bath-bag by
ing dried herbs in a muslin sachet and hanging this under the hot tap.
ven more fragrance is released if it is rubbed on to the body. The bag can
e dried out in the sun and reused until it loses its scent.

Flowers found growing in Cyprus which can be used for this purpose
re **camomile, lavender, rosemary,** and **rose** petals. A therapeutic
inegar bath, for softening the skin and relieving skin irritation, can be
ade by simmering a handful of fresh, aromatic herbs (chosen according
 skin type) with 1 pint cider vinegar for a minute, covering and leaving
 infuse overnight. In the morning the mixture should be strained and
ottled and it is then ready for use — a cupful in each bath.

Herbs which grow in Cyprus
and found useful in skin treatment

Borage	— softening and cleansing
Camomile	— soothing, cleansing and mild astringent
Dandelion	— leaves and roots for cleansing and tonic
Elderflower	— soothing, cleansing and softening
Fennel	— cleansing, gentle astringent
Lavender	— antiseptic
Marigold	— healing and soothing
Mint	— healing, antiseptic
Parsley	— leaves are astringent, and prevent thread vein
Plaintain	— leaves are astringent, cleansing
Coridothymus	— leaves are antiseptic and deodorant
Tuberous Cranesbill	— both skin and eye care
Hypecoum procumbens	— soothing emollient made from the dry flowers
Cape Sorrel	— soothing

PERFUMERY

Strong-smelling flowers such as **lavender** and **roses** can be preserve in oil or alcohol in order to make home-made perfumes.

To make a herbal oil, the chosen herbs are crushed and packed loosel in a glass jar, filled with either olive oil, sunflower, corn or peanut oil. Th mixture is stirred, covered with a piece of muslin and left in the sun for 2-weeks, stirring every day. The oil is then strained and the proces repeated once again with fresh herbs.

Herbs in alcohol are preserved as follows:— take a glass jar with stopper, fill with crushed herbs and cover with pure alcohol. Stop an leave for about one week, strain, and then repeat the whole process onc more.

Some essential or volatile oils cannot be extracted satisfactoril without special equipment. Perfumes made from alcohol were firs distilled in the 14th century. Distillation is expensive and complex toda but the perfumes made at home based on oil or alcohol often have a lighte and more subtle scent. An advantage of alcohol based perfumes is tha they can be diluted with distilled water.

Perfumes made at home should always be stored in air-tight bottles, i a dark cupboard, and the space between the liquid and the stoppe minimal to reduce the harmful effects of air.

A very popular recipe for perfume which has been handed down the ages known as Hungary Water is as follows:—

3 tbsps. rose petals, crushed

3 tbsps. mint leaves, crushed

4 tbsps. rosemary, crushed

1 tbsp. grated lemon peel

$\frac{1}{4}$ pt. (150 ml) orange-flower water

$\frac{1}{4}$ pt. (150 ml) vodka or other alcohol.

The method is simple. Just place all the ingredients in a glass jar fo approximately two weeks, then strain the mixture though muslin anc bottle for another two weeks. This recipe was invented by a Hungariar hermit who gave it to the Queen of Hungary to preserve her beauty.

Another easy recipe for cologne is as follows:—

Rose Petal Cologne

2 cups rose petals, strongly scented variety

2 cups distilled water

$\frac{3}{4}$ cup vodka or other alcohol (odourless)

Place all the ingredients in a glass jar, stir and leave for a few days. Strain and add a few drops of rose oil if a stronger scent is required.

Perfumes can be made from any scented flowers growing in Cyprus using the above methods. If desired, spices such as cloves and cinnamon can be added.

SHAMPOOS

Many shampoos on the market today contain chemicals which are very drying and harmful to the hair. Research is now discovering that herbal ingredients never harm the delicate structure of the hair.

A mild shampoo can be made by mixing two tablespoons of a strong infusion of herbs with two tablespoons of a pure baby shampoo. **Sage** is recommended for dark hair, **marigold** for blond hair and **nettle** for treating dandruff. To give extra body to the hair an egg should be beaten into the shampoo or a tablespoon of powdered gelatine dissolved in the warm infusion.

A scented rinse can be made by adding lavender water to the final rinse. A strong infusion of herbs can be mixed with vinegar or lemon juice to give also a scented rinse. These rinses should always be kept airtight.

Popular recipes used for making hair rinses

Blonde Hair

4 tbsp. dried camomile flowers

2 tbsp. dried marigold flowers

2 tbsp. dried orange flowers

2 tbsp. dried elderflowers

Infused in 1 pint of boiling water and let cool.

Strain and bottle.

Dark Hair

3 tbsp. dried sage leaves
3 tbsp. dried witch-hazel leaves

3 tbsp. dried rosemary leaves

2 tbsps. dried lime

Same method as for blonde hair.

Herbs growing in Cyprus which can be used in shampoos

Camomile — infusion of flowers will soften and lighten the hair.

Marigold — infusion of petals will soften and lighten the hair.

Mullein — infusion of flowers will lighten the hair.

Rosemary — infusion of leaves and flowers will condition, give body and darken the hair.

Goosegrass — infusion prevents dandruff and cleanses the hair.

Lavender — gives scented rinse.

Sage — recommended as rinse for dark hair.

Elderflowers — recommended as rinse for blonde hair.

When reference has been made to an infusion, then standard quantities 15gm/½oz dried herbs or 25gm/1oz fresh herbs to 1 pt. boiling water apply except when other quantities are given.

HOUSEHOLD USE

Herbs can enhance other aspects of our lives adding colour and fragrance to our homes.

In former times, before air-fresheners were invented, folk would hang sweet-smelling herbs from their porches or inside their churches to freshen the air. People also carried pomanders to counteract the evil smells in the air and to combat infection. Now it has been discovered how dangerous aerosols are to the environment, people are becoming interested once again in herbs and many cottage industries are being set-up world-wide making **pot pourries, lavender bags, herb sachets, pillows, moth bags, pomanders, scented candles, furniture polish** and incense.

Pot Pourries

Colourful and fragrant pot pourries please the eye as well as sweeten the air.

Flowers can be collected for making pot pourries at any time of the year. They should be gathered in the morning when the flowers first open. Then they should be spread out on a tray or a piece of wire or hung out to dry in the sun.

Pink or red rose petals usually form the base of the mixture or lavender which is the only other flower that keeps its scent well when dried. Other scented flowers or leaves can be added as well as spices and a fixative such as powdered orris root. Bowls of pot pourri placed at random throughout the house make a delightful addition to one's home.

Flowers and herbs found growing in Cyprus which can be used in making pot pourries are — **Alkanet, borage, marigold, camomile, lavender, mint, mullein, primrose** and the **rose.**

A Simple Recipe for Pot Pourri

600m/1 pt. dried rose petals
600m/1 pt. dried lavender flowers
300m/½ pt. rose buds
150m/¼ pt. bay leaves
150m/¼ pt. rosemary — dried and crushed
150m/¼ pt. marjoram
4 tbsp. each orange and lemon peel
2 tbsps. cloves crushed
6 tbsps. juniper berries
2 tbsps. each allspice, nutmeg, ginger
2 tbsps. orris root
2 cinnamon sticks
2 drops each rose oil and lavender oil.

Store in an airtight jar for 4-6 weeks and use as required.

Herb Sachets

Dried herbs and spices can be mixed inside small cotton bags, trimmed with ribbons or patchwork. Placed on hangers inside your wardrobes they will scent your clothing and keep drawers and cupboards smelling fresh.

Herb Pillows

A larger bag or pillow filled with herbs is said to induce sleep or ease colds. Favourite herbs used for this purpose are **camomile, thyme, mint, rosemary** and **lavender.**

Moth Bags

An excellent deterrent for moths is to mix one cup dried mint with ½ cup dried rosemary, 2 tbsps. powdered cloves and 1 tbsp. lemon peel, the whole being made into small sachets.

Fly Repellents

Several members of the daisy family have antiseptic properties and are used as fly repellents in households e.g. **Tansy, Fleabane.**

Incense

By the 16th Century many common aromatic herbs were collected and burnt to purify and scent a room; Herbs such as **rosemary, juniper, lavender** and **thyme.**

The stalks of dried **lavender** can be used as joss sticks.

Scented Furniture Polish

To add a delightful aroma to your room, ordinary furniture polish can be made to smell sweetly by mixing it with a few dried herbs such as **rosemary, lavender** or **rose** petals.

Candles

Dried herbs added to melted wax before pouring it into moulds will add a delightful fragrance to a room when the candle is lit. The most popular and powerful herb used for this purpose is **rosemary.** Fresh herbs can also be used to decorate candles.

Using dried flowers in so many delightful, imaginative ways can bring a touch of rustic charm to your home. For example a swag of wild flowers adorning a mantlepiece or pelmet can look so attractive. Similarly, a circular garland bedecked with dried flowers hung inside the door also is a pleasing and decorative feature.

It was an early Greek physician called Marestheus who wrote in his book that invigorating herbs such as **marjoram** should be made into garlands for people's guests to wear.

Stunning table decorations can be made from wild flowers using small flower heads to match plates or napkins. A charming effect can be achieved by attaching a small posy of flowers to a plaited ribbon for a pretty napkin ring.

A simple terracotta flower pot or cane basket, both of which are produced en-masse here in Cyprus, can be transformed by adorning the outside with a garland of flowers and packing the inside with an assortment of wild flowers such as **sea lavender** and **helichrysum.**

Another charming way to bring a splash of colour into your home is to decorate a plain straw hat with ribbons and flowers and put on display on either the wall or hat-stand.

I would like to mention that all flowers intended for drying and used in any of the above-mentioned ways should be picked with great discrimination. Herbs should always be gathered before the sun's heat dissipates their essential oils. They quickly lose their scent when they wilt. They should be cut off cleanly and handled as little as possible. Leafy herbs, such as **mint, sage** and **thyme** should be tied in bundles and hung upside down to dry in the sun. All dirty or damaged leaves hould be discarded. Some flowers dry naturally such as the "everlasting" **ea lavender** and **helichrysum.** These should be strengthened with orists' wire before hanging upside down to dry. Large flowers and seed eads can be dried on a piece of chicken wire arranged over a box.

Herbs and flowers usually take between 2-10 days to dry, depending on he humidity and amount of leaf moisture.

Marigolds, pansies, freesias, and **anemones** all respond very well o a process called dessicant drying, retaining their colour and shape. iilica gel is probably the most popular preservative used in this method. also required is a large airtight container. Cover the base with 2.5cms ayer of the dessicant. Lay flower on the surface. Sprinkle the gel over the owers. The flowers should be laid in the container so that they do not ouch and covered with the gel to a depth of 1.5cms. They can be laid out in he sun to dry and are ready when the flowers feel papery. Brush off the xcess gel with a paint brush.

When collecting flowers for drying, please remember to pick them with tmost discernment, giving them the care they deserve for conservation. t is in all of our interests to be circumspect when gathering flowers, by efraining from taking too many within a limited radius and by collecting hem only where that species grows in abundance.

Plants grown in Cyprus with Culinary Uses

Wild herbs have been collected and eaten by man since the earliest times. Each leaf, bud, flower and seed can provide all the minerals and vitamins so often missing from our modern diet. None of the goodness is lost in cooking and furthermore herbs make our food so much more appetising.

Herb flavourings are an essential part of 'al-fresco' cookery so prevalent in the warm Mediterranean climate of Cyprus. It can be merely a few herbs sprinkled on grilled fish or meat or used in making a barbecue sauce to complement the dish. Bundles of **thyme, rosemary, marjoram** and **fennel,** fresh or dried, and bunches of **juniper** and **myrtle** all give a delightful flavour to food. It is the plants found growing close to the sea which compliment fish the most, plants such as **fennel** and **lovage.**

Spices, herbs and honey have been used for sweetening food for thousands of years. Flowers, leaves and whole branches of sweet herbs such as **rosemary, bergamot, lavender** and **marigold** petals can be crystallised and used as sweets. Preserves of jellies and jams are delicious when herbs and spices are added.

Herbs such as **borage, lavender, mint** and **rosemary** can all be used to flavour wine if it is to your taste.

The dried stinging nettles which are so prolific in Cyprus during the summer months are the best packing materials for fruit and root vegetables and moist cheeses. They lose their sting when they are dried and have strong preservative qualities.

Tisanes are very popular with Cypriot folk, using herbs infused for a few minutes in boiling water and then strained. Herbs often used for this purpose are **nettle, sage, camomile** and **elder.**

Fresh or dried herbs can transform the goat cheese made on the island into a delicious gourmet cheese.

Flower vinegars are occasionally used in cookery here as lightly scented flavourings for fruit or cream dishes. The flowers can be left in the vinegar and used for garnishing winter salads. These include **elder-flowers** and **rose** petals.

Culinary herbs suitable for flavouring oils used in dressings and mayonnaise include **rosemary, fennel, thyme** and **marjoram,** and for vinegars, **marjoram** and **mint** are particularly delicious.

Section Two

FLOWERS

PLANTS THROUGH THE SEASONS

On the beautiful island of Cyprus, 1800 species of flowers have been recorded. Approximately 120 of these are said to be endemic. On the following pages I have described for you 100 flowers and 31 shrubs and trees as they appear through the Seasons. The month which I indicate at the top of each page represents the time at which the plant first appears. Listed below are the names of a few of the more popular plants endemic to the island:—

English name	Latin name	Greek name	Page
Troodos Allysum	Alyssum troodi·	Alyssum	101
Wild Pink	Dianthus multipunctatus var. troodi	Dianthus	120
Broom	Genista sphacelata var. crudelis	Raski	139
Onobrychis	Onobrychis venosa	Onobrychis flevothis	93
Chamaepeuce	Ptilostemon chamaepeuce var cyprius	Chamaepeuce	99
Dwarf Carline Thistle	Carlina pygmaea	Karlina	124
Carline Thistle	Carlina involucrata ssp. cypria	Karlina	124
Cyclamen	Cyclamen cyprium	Kyklamino	34
Centaury	Centaurea aegiolophita	Parahosti	95
Wild Thyme	Thymus integer	Livanitis	57
Small-leaved Marjoram	Origanum majorina	Sapsishia	114
Germander	Teucrium micropodioides	Miteres	106
Anatolian Orchid	Orchis anatolica var troodi	Orchis salepi	54
Autumn Crocus	Colchicum troodi	Krokos	29
Crocus	Crocus cyprius	Crokoudi	59
Crocus	Crocus veneris	Krokos	59
Crocus	Crocus hartmannianus	Krokos	59
Common Corn Flag	Gladiolus triphyllus	Agriofrenses	74
Tulip	Tulipa cypria	Toulipa	86

Colchicum troodi (Liliaceae)
Meadow Saffron
AUTUMN CROCUS

Krokos

(V)

In Cyprus this perennial is known as *"Chionistra"* because it is most widespread on the mount of Chionistra in the Olympus range. Both leaves and flowers are poisonous and, in mythology, it is stated that Medea used to grow this plant in Colchida for its emetic qualities. Diosporides said that it was sufficiently poisonous to kill a man in one day. The leaves of **Meadow Saffron** are broad and shiny, growing in a stout cluster in the Spring.

They die back completely in the summer to leave underground corms, hence its other popular name **"Naked Lady"**. The white or pale pink flowers which bloom in the Autumn are usually in groups of 2-5, the long pale stems being the base of an elongated tube which has 6 petal-like lobes at the top. The flowers have a sweet and somewhat mossy scent. It is the female reproductive parts, the "stigmas" or "antlers" which yield the saffron. It takes the dried stigmas of about 4,300 flowers to produce just an ounce of the precious saffron.

In cooking, this is used as a colouring and flavouring agent and in the arts as a dye. **Meadow Saffron** has been used since Classical times to treat rheumatism and gout, for relieving chronic haemorrhaging and faintness. The dose is critical and must be prepared by professionals. Unfortunately, the plant contains an irritant poison which has often proved fatal when taken in excess. It is also very poisonous to cattle.

Location: Mount Olympus and any damp meadowland.

Narcissus tazetta (Amaryllidaceae)
THE POLYANTHUS NARCISSUS

Mitsikorido

(A)

This attactive plant (from the Greek *"narkau"* meaning to grow stiff) is named after Narcissus, the Greek God.

In mythology, he was turned by Hera into the flower.

The flowering season is between November and February. It has several pretty white flowers to a stem and a golden corona, growing to a height of between 25-40 cms.

Attractive to look at, and very fragrant, the villagers like to pick the flowers either for their homes or to sell at the side of the road.

Although the whole plant is actually poisonous, it was discovered in the past to have narcotic qualities and was, therefore, used sparingly as a pain killer and tranquilliser.

Location: Any damp ground e.g. cereal fields and other cultivated land. Common around Dhroushia, Kythrea and Aradhippou.

Muscari parviflorum (Liliaceae)
MUSCARI or GRAPE HYACINTH

**Mouskari,
Agrio Yakinthos**

(R)

This small bulbous perennial, sometimes known as **"Baby's Breath"** is one of several varieties of **Muscari** which grow in Cyprus. This species has faintly scented pale blue flowers and first appears in areas near the sea, soon after the first rains of Autumn.

The bulb lies very close to the surface from which emerge 2-5 grooved leaves and a single flowering stem from 4-20 cms long. 5-20 tiny bell-shaped flowers, less than 5mm. long appear in a single spike.

Location: Sheltered places, appearing first along the coast and later along the roadsides and into the hills.

Bellis sylvestris (Compositae)
WOOD DAISY or MARGARITA

Margarita ton thasson

(A)

This perennial is one of the non-bulbous plants to appear after the Autumn rains and is usually propogated by seeds. The name Daisy comes from "Day's Eye", so named because the flower closes at night, concealing the bright yellow disc at its centre — the sun — and opens again in the morning. The flower also closes in cloudy weather to protect it from any rain or dew which would wet the pollen and prevent pollination.

The plant has a stout root and a rosette of stalked, spoon-shaped leaves which are slightly toothed at the tips. The white ray florets are female and are usually tinged with pink at the tips while the yellow tubular florets in the centre are hermaphrodite.

The plant ranges from 10.30cms in height while the flower heads often appear more than 3cms in diameter.

The **Daisy** is also considered to be useful medicinally as an ointment for treating wounds.

Location: Grassy slopes throughout Cyprus. The foothills below the Kyrenia range.

Arisarum vulgare (Araceae)
JACK'S COWL or FRIAR'S COWL   Koukkoula, Lychnos

(M)

This small perennial with its heart-shaped leaves and spotted stalk has a small tuberous corm which produces many new shoots. As it pushes its way through the ground, it produces a green and white hood, which, with exposure to the sun turns brown and then purple as it withers away.

Hence, its name **"Friar's Cowl"** which resembles the hood sometimes worn by a Friar. In Cyprus the plant is known as *"Koukkoula"* (meaning hood) or *"Lychnos"* (meaning candle) because of its shape. It is also known locally as *"Horton tis Koufis"* i.e. snake grass because of its beneficial use in the treatment of snake bites.

The rhizomes are also thought to be useful in the care of gastritis, catarrh and bronchitis.

Location: widespread, cultivated land, vineyards, damp shady places between rocks e.g. Baths of Aphrodite, the foothills below Kyrenia.

Cyclamen persicum (Primulaceae)
PERSIAN CYCLAMEN

Kyklamino

(R)

This attractive perennial is one of the most widespread and well-loved flowers in Cyprus. The heart-shaped and finely marked leaves first appear in November. They are dark green in colour with greyish patches and white lines resembling lacework. Pinkish-mauve or white blooms follow from December until April. The faintly scented flowers are solitary, swaying at the end of leafless stalks 8-30 cms long with delicate petals turned towards the sky, slightly spiralled, forming a short tube at the base. The *Cyclamen cyprium,* a variety endemic to Cyprus, flowers during the Autumn with leaves which are deep mauvish-purple underneath.

The **Cyclamen** is propogated by its spherical tuber and also by seeds. The tubers which are sometimes referred to as corms are very poisonous. In 50 A.D. Pliny the Elder, a famous Botanist, wrote that **Cyclamen** tubers were used in ancient times to poison arrowheads.

This plant was also found in former times to have medicinal properties and was frequently used to treat rheumatism and arthritis. It was also considered an effective purgative. Today it is used in Cyprus by fishermen for bait.

Location: All shady areas — between the roots of carob and olive trees and rock crevices. Widespread throughout Cyprus but especially on the S.W. coast, particularly Paphos (Tombs of the Kings area) and Baths of Aphrodite.

(R)

THE CYCLAMEN

In open field or leafy bower
The nodding head doth coyly cower
Unshielded from the gentle shower
Sweet Aphrodite's favourite flower
    absorbs the warm Spring rain.

The Cyclamen then to the light
Upraises petals pink and white
To bask in sunshine, Cyprus bright,
Entrancing mortals at the sight
    of stars in bloom again.

Anemone coronaria (Ranunculaceae)
CROWN or POPPY ANEMONE   **Agrioles/Anemone**

(J)

This attractive perennial is very prolific in Cyprus during the winter months. The white variety first appear in December on the lowlands and gradually extend to the highlands. Later on different colours emerge such as pink, red, lilac and purple, the blooms of which will last until April. The flower has five to eight petals protected by three leaves when in bud. The centres of the flowers often have different colours. There are numerous stamens with pink, red or violet filaments and purple antlers.

The flower is very sensitive to light, opening in the sun and closing at dusk. Each stem carries a single flower, 3-7cms in diameter, being very short on dry, hard ground, but reaching 25cms on damp or cultivated ground.

The leaves of the **Crown Anemone** are long and feathery and appear immediately after the first rains, several weeks before the flower emerges. The plant is propogated by its roots.

Location: Grassy slopes from sea level to 1000m.
Common in the Athalassa area, Kambia and the Akamas; the foothills below the Kyrenia range.

Hyoscyamus albus (Solanaceae)
WHITE HENBANE   **Dontochorton**

(A)

This pale green, branched and trailing plant is covered with long, white hairs, making it very sticky to touch. It sometimes grows erect to a height of 20-80cms or more. The flowers are pale green in colour, tubular with a very pale yellow throat. The green calyx remains after the flowers have fallen, turning brown. The flowers appear from December until the end of April.

Another variety of this species which is common in Cyprus is the *"Hyoscyamus aureus* or **"Golden Henbane"** *(Demonaria* in Greek). This plant has brighter yellow flowers with a purple throat.

Both plants contain a poison called Hyoscamine, a substance from which the drug Hyoscine is obtained. In ancient times the plant was well known for its narcotic and analgesic qualities, principally in pain killers and tranquillisers.

Crushed leaves are still used in Cyprus as a cataplasm to reduce pain. Asthma sufferers have been advised to mix the dried leaves of the plant with ordinary tobacco and smoke it like a cigarette. The seeds of the **Henbane** are very poisonous.

Location: Especially areas close to the sea, in rock crevices, along walls of old ruins particularly Makheras Monastery, Tsada, Chloraka in the Paphos area.

Anchusa undulata (Boraginaceae)
LARGE BLUE ALKANET   Melisohorto

(J)

This herbaceous perennial, 30-60cms high, has a thick stem densely covered with white hairs and bristles. Its green leaves are long and spear-shaped also covered in rough, bristly hairs. The bright blue flowers grow in a loose, branched cluster. They have rounded, spreading petals with a tuft of white hairs growing in the throat.

In Cyprus other members of this family can be seen growing at different levels. These include the taller *"Anchusa italica"* with its azure-blue flowers resembling forget-me-nots, and the *"Anchusa strigosa"* which grows as late as May in the highlands and is distinguishable by its paler blue flowers and coarser bristles.

Location: The lowlands in January, later extending to the hills in May.

Romulea tempeskyana (Iradaceae)
ROMULEA

Katsa, Romulea

(A)

This tiny plant, arising from a short stem, 2-3cms long, and bearing 1-5 flowers, can be seen growing amongst the rocks early in the year.

Its funnel-shaped blooms are yellow and purple and will only be found on sunny days as the flowers always close up on cloudy days and after sunset.

The plant is popular with the village children who like to eat the corms which are sweet to taste.

Location: In sandy places between the rocks along the coast.

Silene aegyptiaca (Caryophyllaceae)   **Silene**
CAMPION or
EGYPTIAN CATCHFLY

(J)

This annual has hairy and sticky stems from which emerge a red, cylindrical calyx, and bright pink flowers, 2cms in diameter, orange on the underside. As the flowers wither, the cylindrical calyx turns brown. The whole plant is propogated by seed and the bees are attracted by its nectar. The plant grows to a height of approximately 30cms.

Another variety of this species which grows in Cyprus is the **Bladder Campion** *(Silene inflata)* or more commonly known as *"Strouthi"*. This erect and branched plant has white flowers about 1.5cms across with 5 petals, deeply cleft. It is usually hairless, unlike the **Campion,** and grows to about 90cms high. The bladder is in the inflated calyx tube. The young shoots are often collected by the villagers and are popular fried with eggs.

Location: Both species are common to grassland and along the roadside. The **Campion** can especially be seen in the vineyards around Paphos, Polis, Panayia and Pissouri.

Limonium sinuatum (Plumbaginaceae)

SINUOUS SEA LAVENDER   **Athanato**

(J)

This **lavender** is not related to **French Lavender** (Lavendula species), except in colour, but to the Statice species where dried flowers are often used in flower decoration. In Cyprus it is called *"Athanato"* which means in Greek "everlasting" because, after they are cut, the flowers will retain their colour for a long time, provided they are dried properly.

The attractive blue flowers grow at the end of very strong stems which are protected by soft hairs and will reach a height of 60cms. Due to its very hard root it manages to penetrate deep into the soil for moisture and will continue blooming from February all through the summer until August.

Another variety of **Sea Lavender** *(Statice hyssopifolia), 'Statiki'* in Greek, which grows in Cyprus has much thinner stems and grows never more than 30cms in height. The plants are seen growing in clumps near the sea and the flowers are mauve in colour. They bloom during the summer months from about May.

Location: Abundantly in areas close to the sea.

Matricaria recutita var. coronata (Compositae)
Scented Mayweed
WILD CHAMOMILE

Mouyiochorto
Chamomili

This prolific herbaceous annual which grows to about 25cms appears after the first rains and dies in early Spring. It has white daisy-like flowers with yellow centres which are frequently used when cut and dried, as a herbal drink, promoting peace and tranquillity, and in cosmetics for lightening the hair. It also contains an oil reputed to have anti-allergic qualities, and the plant has been found useful against infections and sore throats.

Location: Widespread throughout Cyprus.

(V)

Taraxacum megallorrhizon (Compositae)

DANDELION

Agriorathiki

This common little perennial has an unbranched stout, hollow stalk, dark brown in colour, from which exudes a milky sap. The flowers are bright yellow, about 3-7cms across, solitary on long stalks arising from a number of leaves. Each floret is strap shaped.

After fertilisation the pappus of soft white hairs is easily dispersed by the wind. It forms the familiar "clock of children's games".

Location: Widespread all over the island.

(J)

Borago officinalis (Boraginaceae)
BORAGE, BEE BREAD

Boratsino

Now native to Cyprus and the Mediterranean area, **Borage** was believed to have originated in Syria. It is an annual herb with hairy leaves and branched stems, and it produces bright blue star-shaped flowers, 2-2.5cms across. It grows easily from seed or by root division and will tolerate some shade. It can grow as high as 30-60cms, and flowers between February and April.

Before the advent of modern antiseptics, an ointment was made for healing wounds by pounding the roots with olive oil and earth worms. The leaves and stems are used medicinally also for rheumatism and, in Paphos particularly, it is well known for infusions to be made to treat colds and pneumonia. The pulped leaves are also used as a poultice for swellings.

The young leaves can be eaten as a salad and they have a slightly bitter, cucumber flavour. The larger leaves can be boiled in the same way as spinach, chopped in stuffings or fried in batter as fritters. The flowers are often eaten raw in salads or may be crystallised as decorations for puddings. **Borage** was said to be a stimulant in times past and "to drive away melancholia". Its chief virtue is as a cooling addition to summer drinks — either steeped with a few young leaves in fruit cups, beer, or wine or frozen in ice cubes.

The roots of **borage** give a grey-green dye when mordanted with alum, and when mixed with oil or alcohol produce a red dye used for colouring liquids, cloth and for staining stones. The red dye was used as a face paint in Ancient Egypt and more recently as a rouge.

Location: Roadsides, wasteland.

(V)

BORAGE

"Begone dull care," declares the Borage
Source of human health and courage;
Think of all its benefits
In drinks and food and cosmetics.
A most rewarding herb this is
It heartens jugs of summer fizz,
It cures all ailments, flavours porridge;
Let's organise a borage forage.

Gynandriris sisyrinchium (Iradaceae)
IRIS   Melanouthia, Irida, Krinaki

This tiny perennial rarely grows taller than 15cms. It is reproduced from bulbs and can be seen during February and March usually in clusters. Two narrow curved leaves appear from the bulb longer than the flowering stem. 2-4 fragrant and very delicate flowers are borne from a stem, each ensheathed in a papery spathe when in bud. The colour of the flowers vary from deep violet to a bluish purple. They open late morning and close as the sun goes down. It is a waste of time to cut these flowers as the blooms will die almost immediately.

Since classical times, the Greeks have used the **Iris** medicinally. A piece of the dry rhizome was often given to babies to chew during teething, acting as an emollient and a sedative. Today, the rhizome is used in modern perfumery and herbal cosmetics.

Location: Dry, stony places of the garigue.

(J)

Iris germanica

FLAG LILY   Krinos

A taller and more robust variety with a thick rhizome and a branched stem reaching about 1m high, can also be seen in Cyprus.

Its long sword shaped leaves are around 2cm wide, greyish green in colour. The fragrant flowers in groups of two or three are about 10cms across. The blooms are purple in colour. The flowering period is longer than the small **Iris** and the flowers can be seen in bloom from March until June in dry, stony places all over the island.

Plantago lanceolata (Plantaginaceae)
RIBWORT PLAINTAIN

Logithes

This perennial herb has long, narrow, ribbed leaves, forming a rosette above a thick root. The tiny brownish, black flowers, 1-2cms, are arranged on tall spikes rising from the centre of the rosette. It flowers from February to May.

In ancient times the Greeks used the plant medicinally in the form of infusions to cure respiratory infections and tuberculosis. It was also used externally to treat injuries.

Location: Widespread in Cyprus.

(V)

Reseda lutea (Resedaceae)
WILD MIGNONETTE

Amouretta

This annual or perennial herb grows to a height of 20-60cms. It is pale green in colour with deeply lobed leaves, a rough, ribbed stem and long narrow spikes of greenish-yellow flowers measuring about 6mm across. It can be seen flowering from February until August.

In former times the plant was used in Cyprus for dyeing material using an infusion made from the flowers. Even today the farmers give their cattle the flowers to eat as a cure for diarrhoea.

Location: Limestone ground, fields, stony areas, especially Kakopetria in the Troodos hills.

Reseda orientalis
WHITE MIGNONETTE

This variety of **Mignonette** has white flowers with 6 petals, the upper pair about 2.5-3mm long and almost as wide. Each flower has 14-21 stamens with filaments 2mm long. The basal leaves are entire, or whole, the upper ones lobed like a palm leaf with 1 or 2 pairs of lobes.

Location: From sea level to 700m.

Viola siechanna (Violaceae)
SWEET VIOLET   **Menexes**

(A)

This perennial can be seen in bloom from February until May and once again in the late Autumn.

It is a creeping herb with dark green, heart-shaped or rounded leaves, larger in the Spring than in the Autumn. The bluish-violet flowers are scented and grow at the end of long stalks, each one solitary to about 10cms high. The flower has 5 unequal petals, the lower petal forming a spur behind. The plant's seeds are usually dispersed by ants.

The **Sweet Violet** contains ionone, a colourless liquid, often used in perfumery. It is said to have a soporific effect. In ancient times the **Violet** was a symbol of humility often depicted in religious paintings. Legend has it that the **Violet** is a symbol of Adam's tears, shed after he was banished from the Garden of Eden.

In Ancient Greece, the **Violet** was a symbol of virginity, its flowers strewn across the nuptial bed.

In medicine, the flowers and roots have been used to prepare infusions for coughs and respiratory complaints.

Since medieval times, candied violets have been consumed as sweetmeats and in the preparation of sherbet.

Location: Widespread throughout Cyprus.

Medicago marina (Leguminosae)

SEA MEDICK

(A)

This perennial can be seen growing prostrate over the sandy shores forming a vivid yellow carpet. It has a robust root which absorbs water from deep under the ground. This enables the creeper to continue blooming during the hot, dry months of summer.

Densely leafy, its stem and foliage are covered by white, woolly hairs. The stem grows from 10-30cms long, branched from the base. The small, pale yellow flowers, about 6mm long, grow in clusters at the end of short stalks and carry a sweet fragrance.

Medicinally, **Sea Medick** has been used to cure anaemia, and to deter bleeding. It has been observed that in Cyprus the flower heads are used to make an ointment for cuts.

Location: In sandy soil along the coast, particularly in the Polis area, Ayia Napa and in the Amathus area.

Mandragora officinarum (Solanaceae)
MANDRAKE, LOVE APPLE
Kalanthropos

(A)

This perennial has dark green leaves up to 36cms long which grow directly from the base of the plant. In February, violet flowers appear in a cluster from the centre of the plant developing into orange-yellow berries about 2-5cms containing a rather unpleasant smell. The root grows to a large size and invariably becomes forked and branched to form a rudimentary human shape. This is why the Cypriots have named it *"Kalanthropos",* meaning "good man". The same name was given it by the Ancient Greeks.

The **Mandrake** is propogated by seed or root division. **Mandrake** is a famous narcotic and has been frequently used in the past as a pain killer during operations. In Biblical times it was thought to induce fertility but as it is also very poisonous, large doses were considered fatal.

Its flowering period extends from February until April.

Location: Common on all wasteland, roadsides and stony places.

MANDRAKE

A shriek of pain to rent the soul	*The schizophrenic Mandrake plant,*
Accompanies the fateful deed	*A 'good man' or a lethal dose?*
Of dragging from its earthly hole	*A medicine when mercy grant,*
This human-rooted Devil seed.	*A poison by the Devil's choice.*

Anagallis arvensis (Primulaceae)
COMMON PIMPERNEL

Mi Me Lismony

(J)

This dimunitive, creeping annual is the blue equivalent of the more well-known **Scarlet Pimpernel** found in other parts of Europe. Although it is usually seen in Cyprus as a blue flower, there is a less-common variety growing on the island in a pinkish-orange shade.

The **Pimpernel** with its small star-like flower blooms from February until June. It opens in the sunshine but always closes up in cloudy weather hence its popular name **"Poor Man's Looking Glass"**. As its flowering period comes to an end, the flower usually becomes larger.

This plant is propogated by seeds — a single plant can produce as many as 500-1000 seeds. These seeds are very toxic.

Location: All cultivated land, gardens, roadsides. Prolific throughout Cyprus.

COMMON PIMPERNEL

Such modesty, such gentle grace
Discouraging inspection,
The Pimpernel needs so little space
to house its' small collection.
Each tiny petal has its place,
Each microscopic section
Forms a shy retiring face
In miniature perfection.

Asphodelus aestivus (Liliaceae)

TALL ASPHODEL

Asphodelos and Spourtoullos

(R)

This herbaceous perennial is very common in Cyprus and can be seen growing to a height of about 1 metre by the roadsides and on any neglected ground.

The sword-shaped leaves, about 60-80cms long, first appear in Autumn followed by flowers in February, on the plains, and three months later in the hills. The blooms appear from branched and leafless stems. The petals are white with a reddish-brown rib down the middle. Another variety of **Asphodel** which grows only in the mountains is *"Asphodeline lutea var liburnica* recognised by its bright yellow flowers.

Throughout the centuries **Asphodel** has been well known for its medicinal qualities, and its root extracts have been used extensively against dermatitis, and today in modern cosmetics. The tubers which are quite edible have been found useful in treating diarrhoea and intestinal disorders. In Cyprus the shoemakers still use the tubers for making glue.

The **Asphodel** flowers are rich in nectar, sweet-scented but if taken indoors give off a strong odour of cats.

In Greek legend it was said that the souls of the dead were fed by the fibrous root of the **Asphodel** and so it could be seen planted on the sites of graves.

Location: Widespread in Cyprus on all uncultivated areas, particularly Paphos area, Polis vicinity, Curium and Episkopi.

(J)

Euphorbia helioscopia (Euphorbiceae)
SUN SPURGE
Galachorton, Galalsitha

(V)

This annual herb grows to a height of 5-30cms and is ubiquitous throughout Cyprus. It has a reddish-brown robust stem with numerous greenish-yellow leaves with slightly serrated edges. The yellowish flowers are arranged in a cluster at the tip of the stems. There is also a trailing variety of this plant in Cyprus called *"Euphorbiamysintes"* which is seen in the mountain areas. The flower blooms from February until May.

A treatise on "Euphorbiaceae", written by King Juba of Mauretania some 2000 years ago detailed the plant's value as a purgative. He named it after his physician Euphorbius and its English name **"Sun Spurge"** is taken from the Latin "purgare" meaning, of course, to purge. In fact, the milky latex which exudes from the stem is highly toxic and, in past times, was used as a cure for warts, scurf and mange.

Even today, some of the islanders use this juice as a rat poison by soaking in it some bread which is then used as a bait. The juice is a very strong irritant and should never be allowed in contact with the eyes or skin.

Location: Cultivated and uncultivated areas throughout Cyprus.

Orchidaceae
ORCHIDS

Kori, Melissa, Salepi

Orchis
italica

(A)

More than 30 species of wild orchids grow on the island of Cyprus. I will describe for you 5 of the more common ones.

Orchids grow sparingly but close together as reproduction occurs mostly by new plants sprouting from the tubers. Reproduction by seed is a very slow process.

One species, the **Bee Orchid** *"Ophrys lutea"*, gets its name from the shape and colour of the bee. It even smells like a female bee and it is reported that in some parts of Europe it is pollinated by the male bee which tries to mate with it. The **Bee Orchid** is found mostly on chalk and limestone and sometimes in dunes and in woods. A rosette of leaves form during the winter months from which a stem appears in the spring reaching a height from 15 to 30cms. This species cannot tolerate disturbance and on no circumstances should be picked.

The **Bee Orchid** is one of the first orchids to appear in the year usually followed by the **Wavy-Leaved Monkey Orchid** *"Orchis italica"* in March and April. The latter is recognised by its pale pink flowers with purple lines borne on a spike about 20cms long. It has long spear-shaped leaves with wavy edges which are sometimes spotted. The flowers resemble little monkeys or men with hands and feet and a forward pointing hood.

At about the same time the **Early Spider Orchid** *"Ophrys sphegodes"* makes its appearance on chalk or limestone and sometimes in sandy dunes. The ones which grow near the sea are generally smaller, sometimes only 5cms tall, and are easily overlooked. Normally they are taller and can carry as many as 8 flowers. Three or four blunt leaves form a rosette from which a single flower stem grows. The flower closely resembles a fat, furry brown spider with a rounded lip and a brown body marked with a blue H.

Also appearing in March, April and May is the **Long-Lipped Serapias** *"Serapeas vomeracea"* known as *"Glossari"* in Cyprus (meaning "tongue"). It is so-called because of its long lip protruding like a tongue. It is a stronger plant than most species, growing to about 50cms in height, with approximately 10 flowers set in a spike. It has narrow, green leaves emerging from 2 tubers. The bracts are longer than the flowers and are brick-red in colour. Each flower has a hood of the same colour with deeply-marked veins.

In April and May, the dainty **Anatolian Orchid** *"Orchis anatolican var. troodi"* can be spotted nestling in the shade of the pine trees on the higher mountain slopes. It grows to a height of between 15 and 30cms. Its bright green leaves, dotted with purple, form a rosette from which emerges a thin flowering stem. The flowers are mauve or pink, occasionally white, packed together on a spike.

An interesting feature of orchids is that they grow in association with fungus in and around their roots. The **Orchid** is a protected plant and once again I emphasise that it should never be picked.

The **Orchid** is no longer used medicinally in Cyprus but in former times infusions from the tubers were made by the islanders for treating diarrhoea and intestinal problems.

Location: The **Bee Orchid** — sandy area, uncultivated land, e.g. Akrotiri, Limassol, and later in the Troodos Mountains.

The **Wavy-leaved Monkey orchid** — grassy slopes especially in the Paphos Area.

The **Early Spider Orchid** — chalk and limestone areas, sand dunes especially Latchi.

The **Long-lipped Serapias** — in grassy areas especially north-west of Paphos and in the Maquis.

The **Anatolian Orchid** — many parts of the Troodos and Kyrenia Mountains.

Ophrys sphegodes   Ophrys lutea   Serapias vomeracea

(J)

BEE ORCHID

Elusive treasure, fragile flower
Hid within some leafy bower,
Tread carefully – that bumble-bee
May in fact an orchid be.

ORCHID

A solitary Orchid
her beauty unbeheld,
But God creates unwasted
every flower in the world.

(A)

Allium neopolitanum (Liliaceae)
NEAPOLITAN GARLIC

Agrioskortho, Skordelli

(J)

This plant is one of the early flowering bulbs, blooming from February until May, to a height of 30-60 centimetres. Its most noteworthy feature is the pungent smell of garlic when the leaves are crushed. The plants are robust with bright green pointed leaves. The buds are enclosed in papery bracts called the spathe which cover the flowers like cupped hands.

A number of white starry flower heads grow from one clump. It is an invasive, dominant plant and often grows in a carpet of white flowers and green leaves. Its properties are similar to those of the cultivated variety, and is still used in Cyprus as a powerful disinfectant, antiseptic and potent protection against disease.

Location: Very prolific on cultivated land, olive orchards and all wastelands and fields, particularly the Pissouri area, Messaoria Plain, Kantara.

Thymus integer (Labiatae)
WILD THYME   **Livanitis**

(M)

This creeping herb has clusters of tiny purple flowers fringed with white bristles. It flowers continuously from end of February until June.

The plant contains thymol, a well known antiseptic and it is said that an infusion of the herb will alleviate diarrhoea.

Location: The rocky slopes of Troodos. Commonly found in the Skarinos area.

Lamium amplexicaule (Papilionaceae)
HENBIT DEAD NETTLE   **Skilakia**

(J)

This small annual herb was named by the Greeks *"Skilakia"* which means puppies in English because the flower has a similar appearance to the mouth of a barking dog. The flower has a pink, velvety texture, appearing first in February and lasting well into April. It is a straggly weed, 15-30 centimetres high and prefers a good quality soil when it can achieve its maximum growth. It has rounded, toothed leaves, the lower leaves long-stalked, the upper leaves half-clasping the stem. The leaves and stem lack the irritant hairs of the stinging nettle hence its name **Dead Nettle.**

The flowers are carried in whorls up the stem at the level of the leaf axil, the whorls having small flowers and being well spaced. Some of the flowers may remain very small, not opening and partly hidden within the calyx. The medicinal properties of **Dead Nettle** have been well known since the Medieval times, being used for respiratory infections and in the treatment of uterus disorders. The villagers in Cyprus still today make **Dead Nettle** tea as a cure for prostatitis.

There is another variety of **Dead Nettle** growing in Cyprus, *Lamium moschatum Mill,* recognisable from the pink species by its white flowers. The flowering period of this variety extends until May.

Location: Wasteland and cultivated land.

rocus cyprius (Iridaceae)
:YPRUS CROCUS   **Crokoudi, Krokos**

This species of crocus is endemic
ɔ Cyprus. It can be seen flowering
rom February to April on the
igher slopes of the Troodos
ɪountains, nestling under the
ines and peeping through the
ɪelting snow.

It has a very small, fragrant
lower, about 8cms high, white to
ale lilac in colour streaked with
rown or purple towards the base.
Two or three flowers usually
merge from one corm which are
ɔnly 4cms across in diameter.

Location: 1200-1950m high in the
Troodos mountains, especially
Prodromos, Chionistra and Ami-
ɑndos.

(A)

Crocus veneris

This variety is similar to the *Crocus cyprius* and also endemic to Cyprus.
It is a delicate flower often to be found in the area of the Tombs of the Kings
and in some villages of the Paphos area.

Crocus hartmannianus

A slightly larger and rare species endemic to Cyprus, growing to about
14-16cms high, the flowers are white or lilac-purple, streaked with dark
purple on the outside. The filaments are orange-yellow in colour. It is located
in the Pine Forest and on stony slopes, from about 750-1000m, especially
Macheras areas.

Ecballium elaterium (Cucurbitaceae)
SQUIRTING CUCUMBER   **Pikragurka, Petragouris**

(A)

A rather strange name for a plant, it was so-called because it bears hairy fruits resembling small cucumbers which, as they mature, change colour from green to yellow. As the ripe fruits fall liquid and seeds squirt out from their interior. The juice which emerges, although rather irritating, is used medically as a cleansing agent.

Extracts from the roots have been used by the villagers for quite some time as a purgative. It is also said to be effective against rheumatism and shingles. The village children find enjoyment in collecting the fruits and throwing them at each other.

The plant itself is a trailing variety, strongly reminiscent of the marrow (or cucumber) with small solitary whitish-green flowers with yellow corollas. The stem is fleshy and the greyish-green leaves are heart-shaped.

Location: Lowland areas on the outskirts of towns and villages.

Tetragonolobus purpureus (Leguminosae)
BIRDSFOOT or WINGED PEA
or ASPARAGUS PEA

Magoutso

This flower is quite prolific through-out Cyprus during the months of Feb-uary to May. It is a hairy annual with branching stems and grows to about 10-30cms. The flower, shaped like a pea, hence its common name, is usually solitary and deep crimson in colour. There is, however, another species which grows in Cyprus called *'Lotus edulis'* whose flower is bright yellow in colour.

Both the flower and stem tops are used medicinally to purify the blood, induce the appetite and as an anti-spasmodic. Children throughout the villages are often encouraged to eat the fresh pods which are claimed to be rich in vitamins and minerals.

(J)

Location: Abundant along waysides especially between Paphos and Polis, wastelands, and fields, particularly near Curium and Kolossi.

Calendula arvensis (Compositae)
FIELD MARIGOLD

Kitrini, Margarita

This common annual, often to be seen with the **Egyptian Catchfly,** grows to about 20-30cms high. Its stems are hairy and small bright orange flowers emerge, about 1-2cms in diameter, from February until about May.

The flower has a pleasant aroma when crushed from which an ointment is made by the villagers for treating wounds and ulcers.

Location: Widespread, vineyards, corn-fields, meadows, wasteland.

(A)

Helichrysum stoechas (Compositae)
EVERLASTING SUN GOLD   **Thakria tis Panagias**

(Y)

This colourful perennial only grows to a height of about 20cms. It is recognisable by its bluish-grey leaves and clusters of mustard yellow flowers which bloom from early February till early April. The flowers are often gathered by flower arrangers and used in dried arrangements similar to **Sea Lavender** and **Grecian Fleabane.** The flowers should be picked before they are fully open and hung upside-down to dry out.

It should be emphasised that these flowers, as with all wild flowers, should only be picked sporadically and with great care in order not to threaten the species.

Location: Coastal areas — sandy soil, rocky hillside.

(R)

Oxalis pes-caprae (Oxalidaceae)

CAPE SORREL or BERMUDA BUTTERCUP

Oxinudhi

(A)

One of the most abundant plants to grow in Cyprus, it makes a splash of brilliant yellow throughout the land in February. **Cape Sorrel** is spread by a creeping rhizome which has clusters of over-lapping fleshy scales below the flower stems. The yellow-green leaves are three-lobed like the clover. Long flower stalks emerge from the centre of the leaves carrying two or more delicate, cup-shaped yellow flowers which only open in the sunshine. It grows to approximately 30cms high. The plant is said to have originated on the Cape of Good Hope from where it spread to the Mediterranean countries and Cyprus.

In the past, the stems were often chewed and eaten by the islanders as the plant contains oxalic acid which gives rather a pleasant taste. It is also used medicinally today as the plant has been found to be effective against skin complaints. It is also found to be used in cosmetology.

Location: Grows abundantly all over the island from sea level to 300-400 metres.

CAPE SORREL

Sybarites in Cyprus are ubiquitous in Summer,
Their floral counterparts appear much earlier in Spring;
Cape Sorrel spreads its' buttercups to sunlight's slightest glimmer,
Not boldly, nor intrusively, but palely loitering.

Leontodon tuberosus (Compositae)
TUBEROUS HAWKBIT or ROUGH HAWKBIT or WILD CHICORY

Agrioradikc

This ubiquitous plant has a bright yellow flower which closes after sunset when you will notice the back of the outer petals have a striped appearance. It blooms throughout the summer and in the dryer regions of Cyprus the plant protects its root from drying out by covering it with its long leaves which protrude from the bass of its hairy stems.

The plant is edible and the Cypriots tend to cook it like chicory, hence its name.

Location: Widespread throughout Cyprus.

(A)

Astralagus lusitanicus (Papilionaceae)
HAIRY MILK VETCH

Kouthounakia or Arkolouthkia

In Cyprus the plant is known as *'Arcovicos'*. This perennial with its clusters of creamy flowers resembling beans can be seen flowering in the lower mountain regions. It grows as a bush up to 1m high, being propogated by seeds. As May approaches the withered flowers produce large pods like broad beans covered with short white hairs.

Location: The East Coast between Limassol and Larnaca, the Troodos Mountains and the North-west coast.

Ranunculus asiaticus (Ranunculaceae)
TURBAN BUTTERCUP
SCARLET or PERSIAN CROWFOOT

Ranunculos

(J)

The colours of this species of **Buttercup** may vary from red, white and yellow tinged with pink. Each flower about 3/6cms in diameter, has shiny petals with a nectary covered by a tiny scale at the base of each petal.

The flowers have 5 green elliptical sepals with tiny hairs on the surface. This buttercup can be seen blooming from February until April up to 30cms high.

A very poisonous plant, it has been used externally only to alleviate rheumatism, arthritis and shingles.

Location: Widespread on hillsides and in the fields — especially in the areas of the Akamas and Akrotiri, and in the foothills of the Kyrenia range.

(J)

Erodium gruinum (Malvaceae)
STORKSBILL

Erodio

(J)

One can observe this common little blue flower growing all over Cyprus during the late winter. It can be recognised by its 5 oval-shaped petals, blue in colour, protected by 5 smaller green and white striped petals.

Each flower is about 2cms wide and emerges from a thick, sparsely hairy stem which reaches about ½m high. Several flowers grow from one stem.

The name **Storksbill** derives from the fruit having beaks 6-7cms long.

Location: Uncultivated land throughout the island.

Trifolium purpureum (Leguminosae)
PURPLE CLOVER

Agrio Triphylli

(V) (J)

This type of **Clover** is very common in Cyprus, a creeping annual which grows to a height of about 20 centimetres. It has narrow, green leaves and the flower heads, oblong in shape are about 2cms long and 1cm wide. The creamy-white petals are pink primarily, turning red later. It is reproduced by both its root and seeds. **Clover** is popular with bees and makes tasty honey. The villagers like to collect the flower heads, dry them and make clover tea which is said to have strong diuretic properties and helps relieve sore throats.

Another variety of clover commonspread in Cyprus is the **Star Clover** *(Trifolium stellatum)*. An annual creeper, also covered in hairs, has flowers ovoid in shape about 3cms wide, forming the shape of a star. It is similar to the **Purple Clover** in that the petals first appear white and turning red later, and it has the same medicinal properties. The **Star Clover** has a shorter flowering period than the **Purple Clover,** appearing usually only in March, whereas the **Purple Clover** can be seen up until May.

Location: Widespread on rocky, sandy soils, fields and hillsides.

Papaver rhoeas (Papaveraceae)
CORN POPPY
FIELD POPPY

Paparouna
Pedinos

(J)

This brilliant red poppy is the one that grows together with the dazzling yellow **Crown Daisy,** forming such a vivid splash of colour across the landscape during March and April.

The **Corn Poppy** grows to a height of about 20cms bearing solitary flowers 7-10cms in diameter. Its milky juice has strong narcotic properties. In olden days, a preparation of syrup from the fruit and flowers was given to sufferers of whooping cough. Today the farmers prepare an eye lotion from the plant to treat their animals' infections.

After the **Corn Poppy** dies down, another vibrant member of the species takes its place, the **Violet-Horned Poppy** *(Roemeria hybrida)*. It is violet or purple in colour with bright green leaves divided into many narrow, pointed segments. It grows to a height of approximately 30cms. A yellow sap exudes from this variety when cut and in the past this was used as an emollient, sedative and painkiller.

In Greek mythology there are many references to poppies. It is reputed that Adonis, lover of Aphrodite, was killed on a hunting trip, and according to legend the poppies are drops of his blood.

Location: Cultivated fields, wastelands. Widespread particularly Paphos, Polis and Kythrea areas.

(R)

POPPIES
Summer parched the yellow grass
Lies injured with the scarlet scars
Of poppies raising up, blood red,
The stab-wound of each blazing head.

Chrysanthemum coronarium(Compositae)
CROWN DAISY

Lazaros, Similloudi

(M)

This very popular herbaceous annual makes a dazzling spectacle of bright yellow contrasting so vividly with the blazing carpet of red poppies prevalent at the same time. Its flowering season usually stretches from December until June but the height of its season is actually March and April.

The **Daisy** is referred to in Cyprus as *"Lazaros"* because traditionally on St. Lazarus Day the villagers pick the flowers for dyeing hard boiled eggs yellow in preparation for Easter.

The plant which is strongly aromatic grows to a height of about 60cms. The flower heads are about 4cms across comprising of a central disc of bright yellow florets surrounded by yellow notched ray florets. As the flower withers and dies the florets turn brown, eventually falling to the ground where they germinate the following year.

Many villagers find the stalks of this plant very palatable. An infusion can be made from the flower heads to treat intestinal complaints. The oil from this plant has been found useful in treating skin complaints, and it has also been found beneficial for rheumatism.

Location: Everywhere in Cyprus. Wheatfields, open cultivation of all kinds, roadsides and wasteground.

(R)

CROWN DAISIES

A fortune lost upon
the ground?
Great hoards of gleaming coins
abound;
Bright golden sovereigns all around.
But greedy eyes my mind confound
For now I see what I have found –
Crown Daisies by the sunshine
crowned.

(V)

Notobasis syriaca (Compositae)
SYRIAN THISTLE   **Aginarohorto, Paparouna, Nerokaulo**

(M)   (J)

This tall, rather unattractive plant is the first of a number of thistles seen growing on the island. This particular variety appears between March and May. It grows to about a metre in height and propogates itself by seeds.

After the flower heads ripen they take on the appearance of soft feathery down which blow away in the wind to propogate for next year.

The flowers themselves are mauve in colour and protected by lethal looking, forked spines.

The thistle is referred to on the island by two names *"Neragantho"* or *"Gaedouragantho"*.

Location: All uncultivated and pasture land.

Alkanna iehmanii (Boraginaceae)
DYER'S ALKANET

Alkanna Asteria, Vaphoriza

(A)

This perennial is of the spreading variety with its stems and leaves densely covered with white thorny hairs. The flowers are bell-shaped, bluish-purple in colour about 6mm long by 3mm wide. It has a thick tap root which turns red when cut and a dark pinkish-red dye has for many centuries been obtained from it to be used in cosmetics. Today it is also found to be used as a natural colouring additive to food.

The islanders refer to this plant as *"Moudoglossos"* and *"Glossa tou Vou"* (meaning tongue of the bull) depending on the region. In olden times, legend has it that if you chew part of the plant and spit it out on a snake the reptile would then die.

Location: Uncultivated fields from sea level to about 900m. Frequently can be found in the Athalassa area.

Gladiolus italicus (Iridaceae)
SWORD LILY/FIELD GLADIOLUS
COMMON CORNFLAG

Macheras
Agriofrenses

(J)

This herbaceous perennial is very prolific in Cyprus and blooms from March until May. In Cyprus the plant is known as *"Paschalia"* because it flowers during Easter (The Greek for Easter is "Paska") or *"Macheras"* (meaning "knife") and sometimes *"Spathohorton"* (meaning sword) because of the shape of its sword-like leaves.

The plant, 40-90cms high is propogated by tiny corms sprouting from the old one. It has an attractive purple flower closely resembling the gladiolus. There is a smaller species on the island called *"Gladiolus triphyllus"* which is similar to a pink freesia in appearance and has 3 bluish-green leaves, hence its name.

Both of the species have been used medicinally for many years. Commandaria wine which is a popular dessert wine produced in Cyprus was found to counteract sterility if the corms from the plant were crushed into powder and mixed with the wine. The farmers also use these corms for feeding their animals which they believe will ensure that they conceive.

Location: Cornfields, orchards, vineyards from sea level to 1400m.

(J)

THE SWORD LILIES

Cool shaded on green mossy banks
A purple-headed army stands;
The sword lilies in serried ranks
Prepare to guard their sovereign lands.

A royal head serenely stoops
And, nodding to his noble peers,
Majestically surveys his troops
Presenting arms of sharp-edged spears.

Convolvulus althaeoides (Convolvulaceae)
CONVOLVULUS or MALLOW-LEAVED BINDWEED   Potirak

(A)

This attractive climber is very ubiquitous in Cyprus and can be seen intertwining clockwise and anti-clockwise over fences, walls and along the banks of roadsides. It flowers from March to May on the hills and to June in the mountains. This perennial has small pinkish-mauve flowers, trumpet-shaped, hence the Greek name for it *"Potiraki"* meaning little glass. In full sunshine the flowers open to a diameter of 3-4cms but as soon as the sunshine fades the flowers close up and die.

The **Convolvulus** belongs to the same family as **"Morning Glory"** *(Ipomea)* which has large blue funnel-shaped flowers and is also very prolific in Cyprus, cultivated mainly in peoples' gardens.

The flowers have a slightly sweet taste and it is known that the villagers give them to their children for constipation. They call the flower *"Fagi tis perdikas"*.

Another variety *"Convolvulus arvensis"* or **"Field Bindweed"** is also prevalent in Cyprus. This creeping perennial has stems up to 1″ long with pink or white funnel-shaped flowers about 15-30cms across. Its leaves are greyish-green and it twists anti-clockwise over other plants. Like other **Convolvulus** the flowers have been used as a purgative, and are made into infusions to counteract constipation. The villagers call this species *"periplokadi"*.

A third species from the Convolvulacea family *"Convolvulus dorycnium"* also can be seen growing on the island. This plant is a hairy upright perennial with a solitary pink and white striped flower on short branches about 2cms in diameter. Its flowering period is short from May to June. As with other **Convolvulus** it is used medicinally by the villagers as a laxative.

Location: Widespread, mainly on lowlands, roadsides, field boundaries, especially Larnaca, Dhekelia, Athalassa, Lakatamia.

(J)

Malva silvestris (Malvaceae)
MALLOW   Molocha

There are two main groups of **Mallow** growing in Cyprus; *'Malva silvestris'* and *'Malva cretica'* or **'Common Mallow'**. The latter, which is a non-hairy plant, usually appears in March followed by the *'Malva silvestris'*, forming bright patches of purplish-crimson until about June. **"The Common Mallow"** is also recognised by its erect hairy stem growing to a height of about 30-100cms.

(J)

Both plants are reputed to have medicinal properties. Pliny declared that any person taking a spoonful of **Common Mallow** will that day be spared from all maladies that might come his way. Pythagorus and his disciples regarded it as good for moderating the passions and cleansing the stomach and mind. Cicero in one of his letters related that he was copiously purged by eating a stem of **Common Mallow** mixed with beet. The **Mallow** is still widely used today in the form of infusions as an effective remedy for intestinal complaints and urinary tract infections. Externally it can be used in the treatment of eye infections, as a gargle for mouth and throat infections and, if fresh leaves of Mallow are crushed in olive oil and applied to bee or wasp stings, the swelling and pain will be reduced.

The **Common Mallow** produces fruits like miniature cheeses, tasting of peanuts which have popular names such as "Bread and Cheese" or "Fairy Cheese". Its edible seeds were what first attracted man to this plant, and then its soft tissues were found to make a good poultice plant.

In the villages in Cyprus the children use the leaves to reduce the pain from stinging nettles. In former times, the monks at Stavrovouni monastery survived on the shoots of **Mallow** during Lent. The plant is very common in that area.

Location: Wasteground, cultivated fields, olive groves and citrus plantations, widespread.

alvia fruticosa (Labiatae)
AGE

Faskomilo, Spatzia

The smell of this perennial herb can be enjoyed all over the hills of Cyprus. It blooms from March until June with small purple flowers and greyish-green leaves hairy underneath and wrinkled above. The bush grows to a height of about 0.8 metres.

The leaves of **Sage** are collected and used for making tea in Cyprus *"Spaja chai"*. They are also very popular in cookery and have been found a useful aid to digestive problems. **Sage** flowers, with their fragrant resin, were used to make a cordial which, in the 17th century, was believed to make men strong and to retard the rapid progress of decay.

The name *"salvia"* derived from the Latin *"salvare"* means "to save" or "to cure" and has become a highly esteemed medicinal plant. Its virtues are said

(A)

to be manifold — as an aperitif, a tonic, a mouthwash, a cure for eczema, combats dandruff, for rheumatism, gout and sciatica, asthma and diarrhoea.

On the island it is commonly referred to as *"Hahomilia"* and *"Alisfakia"* and *"Spaja"*.

Location: Widespread particularly in the Troodos Mountains.

Tanacetum vulgare (Compositae)
TANSY or BATCHELORS' BUTTONS   **Katerina**

(V)

This plant is not very common but can usually be found up in the mountains close to a spring. The button-shaped flower heads are composed of a tightly-packed cushion of tiny yellow tubular florets with a sunken dimple in the centre of each flower head.

"Athanasia" was a name given by the old Greek herbalists to this plant. In Greek it means "immortality" which probably refers to the everlasting qualities of the dried plant, to its medicinal properties or to its use in embalming corpses.

In Cyprus the name *"Katerina"* was given to the tansy by the villagers of Platres in the Troodos Mountain.

Location: Troodos Mountains.

THE TANSY
The Tansy may be hard to find
Immortal in its grace,
But buttons from bold batchelors!
Distinctly out of place!

Geranium tuberosa (Geraniaceae)
TUBEROUS CRANESBILL

Yeranium

(P)

This perennial reaches a height of 20-40cms. Its leaves are greyish-green and finely divided. The flowers are saucer shaped, pinkish-purple in colour with darker veins and measure approximately 1½cms across.

Each flower has stamens about 3mm in length with oblong antlers.

In the past the plant has been used medicinally as a diuretic, an astringent and in skin care.

Location: Widespread especially in the Akamas area.

Hypecoum procumbens (Papaveraceae)

ST. JOHNS WORT

Paparounia

(A)

This plant is an erect or creeping annual about 10-30cms high with bluish-green leaves, narrowly divided. The single yellow flowers appear on short stalks about ½—1½cms across. Each flower has 4 petals.

In times past the juice from the stem has been used as a sedative.

In Cyprus the villagers have used the dry flowers to make an emollient for the skin and as a sedative for coughs and respiratory problems.

Location: Widespread, cultivated and uncultivated land particularly in the Nicosia area.

Hypecoum imberbe
ST. JOHNS WORT

Paparounia

This plant is very similar to *Hypecoum procumbens* in general appearance but with the divisions of leaves usually narrower, and the bracts less conspicuous.

The flowers are larger, usually orange-yellow, the petals being 3-lobed 1cm in length and width.

(A)

Ranunculus muricatus (Ranunculaceae)
CREEPING BUTTERCUP

Provataris

In early Spring, March to April, this spreading buttercup can be seen in any damp ground. It has small pale yellow flowers with spreading sepals and long, stalked shiny leaves.

The **Buttercup** has been used medicinally in the treatment of dermatitis and rheumatism but, as it is extremely poisonous, it has only ever been used externally in the form of a tincture.

Location: Throughout Cyprus where the ground is damp.

(V)

Leontice leontopetalum (Berberidaceae)
LEONTICE

Voidokratis, Tsakra

This perennial is an erect, herbaceous perennial about 20-50cms high. It grows from a bulb with a leafy stem bearing long-stalked yellow clusters of flowers in the axils of their bracts. The leaves have three lobes and are blue-green in colour. It flowers throughout March and April.

The bulbs or tubers of this plant have been used extensively in the past for treating migraine and epilepsy. It is still today used for making soap due to its detergent qualities.

Location: Cultivated land, most common in the wheatfields.

(A)

Legousia speculum veneris (Campanulaceae)
VENUS LOOKING GLASS

Agria Yioulia

This small annual gives a vivid display of bright purple in the open fields during March and April. The small flowers are only about 1.5cms in diameter and grow about 10-15cms high.

The name is said to derive from the seeds which are oval, flat and highly polished, but would make a very small mirror for Aphrodite to admire herself in.

Location: Open fields all over Cyprus.

(V)

Scabiosa prolifera (Dipsaceae)
SCABIOUS   **Scaviosa**

(A)

There are several species of **Scabious** growing on the island. The first to appear during March have cream flower heads about 3-4cms in diameter, resting in the forks of branches which grow to about 20cms high. It is commonly known as **"Carmel Daisy"**.

Later in the summer another variety appears on the higher mountain *(Scabiosa crenata)*. The flowers are pale lilac and the spindly plant grows to a height of about 3 feet. The flowers are known to have a strong attraction for bees.

The botanical name *"Scabiosa"* is derived from the reputed power of some of the plants of this species to cure scabies and other skin conditions.

Location: **Carmel Daisy** — wastelands, and roadsides.
            Lilac scabious — mountain slopes.

Tulipa agenensis (Liliaceae)
WILD TULIP

Toulipa

(S)

This colourful **tulip** blooms in a vibrant red with yellow and black centres. It is commonly referred to as the **"Sun-Eyed Tulip"**. The buds first appear in March in the same colour as the leaves, and the flowers continue to bloom until May. After nightfall the petals close up.

New plants are reproduced from new bulbs which appear next to the parent bulb.

Location: Cultivated fields, particularly in the Stroumbi and Polemi area near Paphos.

Tulipa cypria

This variety of red **tulip** is endemic to Cyprus. It is quite prolific along the roadsides in the Akamas area.

Unfortunately, both species of these **tulips** are in danger of eradication in Cyprus due to deep ploughing, indiscriminate use of herbicides and frequent picking before the flower seeds have developed and the flowers had time to spread.

Tragopogon sinuatus (Compositae)
SALSIFY or VEGETABLE OYSTER
or PURPLE GOATSBEARD

Kalakatsouna

(J)

This perennial grows widespread in Cyprus and the islanders use it as a vegetable and to flavour their salads as both its tap root and leaves are edible. It is recognisable by its pale pinkish-violet flowers with green bracts spread out under each head like a star.

Although it can grow to a height of 60cms it often goes unnoticed as its flowers only stay open for a few hours each day. This plant comes from the same family as "Yellow Goat's beard" or "Jack-go-to-bed-at-noon" named because of its habit of closing its flowers at noon.

The family *"Trapogon sinuatus"* is common to Western Europe. it was known to Dioscorides as *'Barba hirci'* which is translated as "Goats beard". Before the seed head develops, the pappus or ring of feathery hairs which surround the seed closely resembles a beard.

The head develops into a huge "dandelion" to be dispersed by the wind.

Location: Uncultivated fields and roadsides throughout Cyprus.

Orobanche crenata (Orobanchaceae)
SCALLOPED BROOMRAPE or
BRANCHED BROOMRAPE

Likos

(M)

This plant is very unpopular in Cyprus due to the fact that it is a parisitic plant. It lacks its own green leaves and stems and therefore lives off vegetables, especially peas, and crops are seriously affected.

It is recognisable by its creamy, white flowers, arranged in a form of a spike on a thick, dark red stem which is densely covered with fine brown hairs.

It can be seen growing during the months of March to June and may exceed 60cms.

Location: All cultivated fields.

Ornithogalum pedicellare (Liliaceae)

STAR OF BETHLEHEM   Asteri tis Vithleem

(J)

There are several varieties of this species growing in Cyprus. The plant blooms from small bulbs with white and yellow flowers. This short, spreading plant has narrow, limp, grooved leaves, 1-4mm wide, with a central white stripe.

The star-like flowers, about 2cm in diameter, have 6 petals with a green stripe on the back of each petal, 6 yellow stamens, and each flower forms an umbel-like cluster on a leafless stem.

"Ornithogalum chionophilum" is a slightly larger species found growing on Chionistra in the Troodos mountains.

Location: Dry, rocky slopes of the hills and mountains.

STAR OF BETHLEHEM

'O, little town of Bethlehem
how still we see thee lie.'
As children we have praised thy star
in Christmases gone by:

Now when we see this floral shape
with contemplative mind,
Those songs of innocence recall
that world we left behind.

Cynoglosum creticum (Boraginaceae)
HOUNDS TONGUE   **Kynglosso**

(J)

This hairy biennial with erect stems and grey leaves clasping the stem, grows to a height of about 45cms. The flowers measure approximately 7-10mm across borne on separate branches.

Each flower has 5 petals and stamens, the petals being pale blue with violet veins. It can be seen blooming between March and May.

In former times this plant was used medicinally to cure lung infections.

Location: Widespread on wasteland and cultivated fields.

Cichorium divaricatum (Compositae)
DWARF CHICORY   **Agrioradiko**

This much-branched annual with its tough stems and blue-green leaves similar to the Dandelion, reaches a height of about 30-70cms. Its flowers are clear, sky blue, 2-4cms across and is propogated by seeds. You will notice the flowers only open in the morning as in the afternoon its petals appear to droop.

The villagers like to boil the leaves and digest them for their medicinal qualities. The plant is reputed to cure a number of digestive problems, is beneficial to the liver and will act as a purgative.

Dioscorides recommended it as a cure for burning and upset stomachs. The stout tap roots are roasted and ground and blended with coffee or used as a coffee substitute.

Th Cypriots call the plant *"Pikralida"* from the Greek *"Pikros"* meaning bitter.

(V)

Location: All over Cyprus on wasteland, pastures, roadsides and boundaries.

DWARF CHICORY

A brief display
of blue each day
Is like to be
Dwarf Chicory.

Perhaps it knows
That we propose,
(Though flowers waste)
It's roots to taste.

Viola sieheana (Violaceae)
COMMON DOG VIOLET   **Agrios Menexes**

(V)

   This plant, a perennial, only grows to a height of about 3-20cms. It has a hardy rootstock, an erect stem from which emerge rather large leaves, long or oblong arising from a loose rosette and on the end of long stalks.

   The flowers are solitary, bluish-violet in colour, with 5 petals, the lower one showing black lines towards the centre. They do not have a scent.

   Since medieval times, the plant has been used medicinally as a diuretic and externally for the treatment of rashes and spots.

Location: You can find the plant growing in April and May in stony areas from 750m high to 1950m.

Onobrychis venosa (Papilionaceae)
ONOBRYCHIS   Onobrikis Flevothis

(A)

One of several species to be seen growing on the island, this particular variety, endemic to Cyprus, can occasionally be seen amongst the limestone hills and rocky areas along the coast. The pale, creamy coloured flowers shaped like peas are about 1cm long growing in clusters of about 4cms long.

Each cluster is carried on a long stem about 15cms long. The dark green leaves are striped and velvety in appearance and covered in short, fine hairs.

Another variety to be seen in Cyprus is called *"Onobrychis crista galli"* which has bright pink flowers growing on slightly shorter stalks.

Location: Onobrychis venosa — lowlands in limestone soil and along the rocky coastline. *Onobrychis crista-galli* — widespread in Cyprus; fields, hillsides.

Paeonia mascula (Paeoniaceae)
PEONY   Paeonia

(A)

This perennial which grows to approximately 30-60cms has thick woody roots, purplish-red stems and leaves which are bright green on the top and dull bluish-green underneath. The pink tulip-like flowers are about 10cms across, opening at the end of April for about 3 weeks.

They have a faint aroma of cloves. Each flower is solitary and, similar to other members of the Ranunculaceae family, will only open in the sun.

It is said that **Peony** was brought to Cyprus by medieval monks for its medicinal uses. The peony has been used since the Middle Ages as a painkiller and tranquilliser. Homer said that Peon, the healer of Gods, used this plant to treat Plato.

Location: Mountain areas about 1350m; the pine forests in the Troodos Mountains, at Prodromos, and on the lower slopes in the vicinity of Madhari.

entaurea aegiolophita (Compositae)

ENTAURY KNAPWEED   **Parahosti**

(A)

This stemless herb is one of the first thistles to emerge in Cyprus during the spring and it continues to grow until about August.

The plant is anchored to the ground by a long tap root. The leaves vary in shape and fan out along the ground in a rosette shape. The flowers, 5cms across, are sometimes creamy in colour and sometimes pink.

Known locally as *"Parahosti"* (meaning hidden away), the plant enjoys sandy soil and sometimes stays half buried.

In the past the villagers have used the flowers to make an infusion for treating eye complaints. It has also been used for indigestion and as a diuretic.

Location: Sandy areas along the coast especially Latsi, near Polis and on the rocky slopes of the Troodos Mountains.

Allium ampeloprasum (Liliaceae)
WILD LEEK

Agrioprass

This sturdy plant grows to a height of approximately 1m. It has a strong garlic smell and grows from a bulb with many bulbils. The flower heads form a dense round cluster of lilac flowers with protruding stamens and yellow antlers. Each flower head measures approximately 10cms across.

You can find it flowering in cultivated fields and wasteground during the months of April and May.

In former times, the **Wild Leek** was popular as a vegetable and in medicine for its diuretic qualities.

Location: Common all over Cyprus

(M)

Corydalis rutifolia (Fumariacea)

Hionistra

This small perennial related to th fumitories has delicate pink flower and tips of a deeper pink similar to th orchard in appearance. Its blue-gree leaves appear in pairs divided into : leaflets on short stalks. During th summer and winter months the plan rests underground as a small tube about 3-5cms wide. Then in April th first leaves appear followed by th flowers.

The tubers of this plant has bee used in medicine to treat nervou disorders.

Location: The highlands, mainly Moun Olympos in the Troodos Mountains.

(J)

Delphinium peregrinum var. eriocarpum (Ranunculaceae)

LARKSPUR

Linarida, Karfohorto

This little annual only grows to a height of about 30-50cms. It grows quite sparingly and is very fragile. It has violet-blue, pink or white flowers and is propogated by seeds. It flowers from April to July.

This flower has been used in medicine for years, particularly as an ointment for psoriasis. Some of the villagers call it *"psorochorton"* meaning *"psora"*-*psoriasis* and *"chorton"-herb*. It was also found valuable as a diuretic.

Location: Pastureland and roadsides, particularly in the Akamas area and in the Athalassa forest.

(Y)

Pallenis spinosa (Compositae)

PRICKLY OXEYE

Spalathia

Up to 60cms high, this softly hairy plant has hard, branched stems, spear-shaped leaves, and bright yellow flowers, 1-2cms in diameter shaped like the daisy. It is recognised by its whorl of green, spiny bracts under the flower-head, spreading out like a star.

The flowers usually turn brown as they die. They normally continue blooming until the middle of June.

Location: Widespread throughout Cyprus in the lowlands and the highlands.

(J)

Muscari comosum (Liliaceae)
TASSEL HYACINTH

Agriohyacinthos

(J)

This large **hyacinth** is characterised by its striking tassel of bright blue flowers emerging from widely-spaced purplish-green flowers.

The bees are initially attracted by the blue sterile flowers but find they lack nectar and move down to the greenish flowers to feed. Each bulb, 3cms in diameter, produces 2-3 narrow pointed leaves up to 1.5cms wide and 50cms long. The flowering season usually lasts about 1 month.

The bulbs have been found to have antiseptic and healing qualities and are also edible. Their bulbs are still eaten today by some of the villagers. It is believed that they lower one's cholesterol level.

Location: Cultivated and uncultivated land, appearing first in the lowlands and extending later to the hills. Often seen in vineyards and orchards.

Ptilostemon chamaepeuce (Compositae)
CHAMAPEUCE

Kirsio, Chamapeuse

(Y)

This much-branched bush grows to a height of about 80cms. It has long thin leaves, dark green on top and white underneath. It closely resembles the **Syrian Thistle** with its purple flowers surrounded by bracts which appear at the end of long stems.

The **Chamapeuce** has been used medicinally since former times in the treatment of arthritis and rheumatism.

Location: Along the roadsides and in the hills where it is dry and rocky. Especially the lower Troodos hills. Common in Kakopetria and Marathasa area.

Tordylium aegyptiacum (Umbelliferae)
TORDYLIUM or HARTWORT

Tordilio

This is an attractive annual with groups of very small white flowers growing at the end of branched stems, reaching a height of about 50cms.

The disc-shaped green seeds known as *"psomouthkia"* (small bread) have been eaten in the past by the villagers to combat indigestion. An extract from the seeds has also been used to help cure jaundice and also as a diuretic.

In Cyprus you will hear the plant referred to as *"Melissantros", "Pitsikliantros"* or *"Kankalithres"*.

Location: In both cultivated and uncultivated fields.

(M)

Echium italicum (Boraginacea)
ITALIAN BUGLOSS

Ekion to italicum

The name **"Bugloss"** from the Greek *"Vous Glotha"* or **"Cow's tongue"** is a reference to the shape and bristly texture of the leaf. This plant was linked from Ancient Greek times with snakes. In August the fruits harden into four nutlets which were supposed to resemble a snake's head and as a consequence were used to treat snake bites.

In appearance the whole plant resembles a Christmas tree when dead or dying as it is covered in bristly white hairs giving it a frosted look. During April the spike is composed of many curled clusters each producing small flesh-coloured trumpet-shaped flowers. It is often seen growing with the **Common Mallow** on the roadsides to a height of about 1m.

Location: Grassy banks, roadsides particularly around Limassol and Platres in the Troodos Mountains.

Galium aparine (Rubiaceae)
GOOSEGRASS
CLEAVERS Kollitsida

This annual is a hedgerow plant which scrambles and clings to other vegetation often in dense masses. It has minute hooked bristles which often cling to animal fur which helps the seeds to disperse. The flowers are greenish-white, arranged in clusters of 2-5 at the end of long stalks.

In times past the plant was fed to geese hence its name. It is still used medicinally in Cyprus in the external treatment of wounds and ulcers.

Location: Widespread along the roadsides.

(V)

Alyssum troodi (Cruciferacae)
ROCK CRESS or TROODOS ALYSSUM Alyssum

This species of plant, endemic to Cyprus, grows only in the mountains, mainly on the north-facing slopes. It resembles the Golden Alyssum seen in European rock gardens. Its tiny, bright yellow flowers, about 3-4cms across, and its blue-green pointed leaves make a strong contrast against the bleak, rocky surface of the mountains. Its season is fairly short from mid-April on the lower slopes to June in the higher mountains.

(Y)

The old Greek word for rabies is *"Lyssa"* and the plant was reputed in former times to cure the disease. Hence its title **"Alyssum"** meaning 'against rabies'.

Location: Troodos Mountains.

Centranthus ruber (Valerianacea)
RED VALERIAN   Kentrantho

This herb is only to be found on the higher slopes of the mountains in Cyprus as it grows best in cool weather. It grows to a height of about 100cms and has a number of small red flowers growing in clusters at the end of each stem.

Location: Rocky places such as Troodos mountains, particularly in Platres.

Valeriana italica
PINK VALERIAN

This pale pink variety of **Valerian** is to be found on the lower slopes and in coastal areas. It flowers from February to May and can often be found in the crevices of boulders.

(J)

Gagea graeca (Liliacea)
LLOYDIA   Loutia

One tends to think of lilies as tall-stemmed with large white flowers. This species, however, is a tiny plant with solitary, delicate white flowers, only growing to a height of about 16cms. The flowers are slightly cup-shaped, growing on thin stems with narrow grass-like leaves.

Location: Lime soils especially in the Limassol district.

(Y)

Jerbascum sinuatum (Scrophulariacea)

MULLEIN

Phlomos

A tall, stately plant this biennial reaches a height of between 50 and 100cms. It is easily recognised by its rosette of thick leaves, covered with silvery down and, during the second year, by its flowering spike of bright yellow flowers with orange antlers. It can be seen flowering from May through to July.

Both the flowers and roots have been used medicinally in the past especially as infusions for respiratory problems. Also, if the flowers are steeped in olive oil, and left in the sun for two weeks, then strained, the lotion can be used for massaging aching joints.

In former times the down from the stems used to be rubbed and dried for use as tinder and lamp wicks.

The leaves can also be boiled and used as a poultice for skin infections.

In Cyprus, villagers still feed their cattle on dry **Mullein** roots as a cure for diarrhoea and other intestinal problems.

(V)

Location: Grassy slopes and dry areas of Cyprus. Common throughout the island.

MULLEIN

The striking flower of Mullein
stands tall above the rest
With brilliant yellow petals
round a scarlet centre-piece
And just to show its' neighbours
that it really is the best,
Its' foliage and stems display
exclusive Golden Fleece.

Artemesia arborescens (Compositae)
WORMWOOD   Yenia tou gerou

This perennial herb, growing to about a metre high is recognised by its whitish-grey leaves and small yellow, nearly globular flower heads arranged in a cluster like the mimosa. The leaves exhale a strong, aromatic odour when crushed between the fingers. Its season is short from May until June.

Its virtues have been known since ancient times. Galen advocates it as a powerful tonic, Avicenna as a remarkable stimulant to the appetite. The Salernitan School recommends it as a preventative against sea-sickness, adding that *"it soothes the stomach and the nerves"*, expels worms and mitigates the effects of any poison that may have been drunk. It is said to have the power of eliminating gases from the stomach and is recommended for bad breath caused by stomach disorders. It has also been employed as an eye lotion for diseases of the eye.

A further use has been in the past to regulate the menstrual cycle. However it is pointed out in several books on herbal medicine that wormwood — which forms an ingredient of the drink called "Vermouth" —should never be used for too long (8-10 days at the most) because its therapeutic effects would become nil and it can give rise to an irritation of the gastric mumosa and affect the nervous system.

Location: Along hedgerows and walls especially in the Nicosia area, Makheras Monastery, Kalopanayiotis, Kythrea.

WORMWOOD
With such an unattractive name
The Wormwood plant deserves more fame.
Considering its' noble past,
with well-known herbs it should be classed.
In medicine it brings a wealth
Of benefits to our good health,
Producing from its' flavoured leaf
a popular aperitif.

Cynara scolymus (Compositae)
GLOBE ARTICHOKE

Anginara

(M)

This perennial can reach a height of 150cms and resembles a thistle. The greyish-green, tightly over-lapped floral bracts form a rounded or conical head up to 12cms across from which small, pale purple florets emerge.

The edible flower heads should be removed while still in the bud stage. You often see the villagers in Cyprus chewing on the buds as they work in the fields. They may be boiled and served hot or cold. The edible parts of the flower head are the fleshy base of each scale and the artichoke heart, which is at the bottom of the flower has the finest flavour. The hearts are often extracted and served on their own. The young leaf shoots known as chards are edible and used like celery.

Location: Sheltered positions in cultivated fields.

Cynara cardunculus

This plant is abundant in the Mesaoria region where it appears to be, if not wholly indigenous, at least completely naturalised. It is less popular in cultivation than the *Cynara scolymus*.

Plants grown from seed are said to revert to the more spiny *Cynara cardunculus.*

Teucrium micropodioides (Labiatae)
GERMANDER

Miteres

(M)

This rather small perennial shrub, with its many branches, can be seen growing to a height of about 10-20cms.

Its branches are covered with white hairs and the leaves which are greyish-green in colour, are from 4-10mm long by 1.3mm wide. The corolla is purple or red about 3.5mm long by 1.5mm wide. This endemic species is fairly common in Cyprus and flowers from early May until July, sometimes earlier.

The plant has often been used in medicine as an effective remedy for jaundice, stomach complaints and as a diuretic.

Location: On dry rocky areas mostly and occasionally seen on the beaches. Very common in the Akamas, Athalassa, Protaras and Dherenia areas.

inguicula crystallina (Lentibulariaceae)
BUTTERWORT

(A)

The members of this family are insectivorous plants of water and wet places. This particular species is said to be endemic to Cyprus and can only be seen growing in the Troodos Mountains such as streams and on the edges of waterfalls. Its very pale, violet flowers with yellow centres can be seen peeping out of the clefts of wet rocks. Each flower is solitary, borne from thin, leafless stems protruding from a rosette of greenish-yellow leaves. The leaf surface is covered with minute glands which exude a sticky liquid, trapping insects and digesting them. It grows from 6 to 10cms high.

In the 15th and 16th centuries **Butterwort** was used in Europe as a milk-curdling agent, hence its other name "thickening grass", and also as an ointment for curing sores on cows' udders, and as a result the plant became known as **"Butterwort".**

Location: Troodos Mountains.

BUTTERWORT

On Troodos mount in ambush lies
This cruel plant with violet eyes.
Innocent insects, gathering round
Seductive blooms in marshy ground,

Alight upon adhesive leaves,
To find – too late – how sight deceives.
Carnivorous Butterwort, thou wert meant
For loitering with foul intent.

Lantana camara (Verbenacea)
SPREADING
SUNSET   Lantana

This evergreen shrub is said to have originated in the West Indies. It reaches a height of between 40 and 120cms and spreads between 30 and 100cms. The egg-shaped leaves are mid-deep green. The flowers which are prostrate, are borne from the leaf axils in domed heads about 5cms across. They are produced from May to October and range from white through to yellow-brick red. The flowers often darken as they age so that two or more colours can be seen in one head.

Location: Widespread throughout the island.

(J)

Vicia cassia (Papilionacea)
VETCH

Vikia or Agriovikos

This plant can be seen climbing over rocks and stones during the summer months. It has long, green tendrils and small mauve flowers about 1-2cms long growing in pairs and resembling peas in appearance. It is propogated by seeds.

Location: Dry and rocky places.

(J)

colymus hispanicus (Compositae)
PANISH OYSTER PLANT   Chrisangatho

(Y)

This spiny plant resembles a thistle with its yellow stalkless flower heads overtopped by very spiny bracts.

It grows from about 20-80cms high and has hairy stems and leaves with wavy margins and strong spines. The golden flowers are stalkless growing from the axils of the leaves and grow regularly along the stems.

Each flower is approximately 1½ cms broad with 5 stamens and yellow antlers.

You will find the **Spanish Oyster** flowering in Cyprus from June, sometimes early as May, until August.

Location: Common all over the island on wasteground and sandy areas mainly in the lowland areas.

Centaurea hyalolepis (Compositae)
PALE STAR THISTLE   **Athratsides, Trisakida**

(J)

   This low spreading herb is one of the first thistles to be observed as the summer approaches. It has bright yellow flower heads with spines forming a star beneath. The flower is solitary about 6cms across. It is rich in nectar and a valuable source of honey for the bees.

   The plant contains centaurin which has been used in medicine as a diuretic, purgative and digestive, and as an infusion externally for eye inflammations. The villagers also use the herb in cooking, boiled and served with oil and lemon juice.

Location: Cultivated and uncultivated ground, roadsides. Common all over Cyprus.

Eryngium creticum (Compositae)

ERYNGO   **Pangallos**

(Y)

This spiny plant, 50-80cms high, has stems and leaves tinged with violet. The lower leaves are heart-shaped and the upper ones are divided into narrow spiny segments. The flowers are blue about 0.5-1cm across. There are 5 bracts surrounding each flower head, 3-5 times longer than the globular flowers.

It can be seen mainly in the lowlands during May through to September.

In Cyprus this plant is commonly used as a vegetable. Its lower leaves are often pickled and eaten in salads. The roots have frequently been used as a treatment for snake bites.

Location: Wasteland, grassy and stony. Very common in the Larnaca, Kythrea, Polis and Lymbia areas.

Cardopatium corymbosum (Compositae)
CARDOPATIUM

Opyros

(M)

This short-stemmed and many branched plant, growing to about 25cms. high, consists of clusters of bright blue flowers surrounded by very spiny leaves.

It is seen growing in sandy areas along the coast.

In former times, **Cardopatium** was used medicinally as a painkiller and for stomach ache. Dioscorides recommended it for toothache.

Location: Common along the beaches and dry areas further inland. Particularly seen at Ayia Napa, Yeroskipou and in the Akamas.

Hypericum perforatum (Hypericacea)
PERFORATE ST. JOHN'S WORT
COMMON ST. JOHN'S WORT

Balsamohorto, Prodromos
Psillina

This erect and branched perennial grows to a height of about one metre with alternate leaves on which are seen tiny, translucent dots. The flowers are yellow, about 2cms across, with 5 petals and small, black dots around the margins. The long stamens are tipped in red. The flowers are quite prolific on every plant.

Perforate St. John's Wort acquired its name because the oil glands within the leaf extends almost from surface to surface giving the appearance of little holes. This oil gives off a lovely aroma and the leaves are often used to scent clothes cupboards. They also act as a good moth repellent. The essential oil is extracted by soaking its flowers in olive oil. This has been found most useful in treating burns. An infusion has also been prepared for treating external wounds and injuries in order to speed the healing process.

(A)

Another member of the **St. John's Wort** family which can be found on the island is *"Hypericum triquetrifolium"* also referred to as *"Psilliana"* by the villagers. This is an annual, growing to about 50cms, with a much branched stem. Its flowers are smaller, about 1cm wide but the number of flowers on each branch are just as numerous. Its flowering period is longer than the **Perforate St. John's Wort** from May to September. The latter can only be found during the month of June.

Location: Hypericum perforatum — woods, cultivated land and hillsides from about 600 to 1500m.
Hypericum triquetrifolum — cultivated land, sandy soil or dry and stony ground to about 1400m.

Origanum marjorana (Labiatae)
SMALL-LEAVED MARJORAM   **Rigani, Sapsishia**

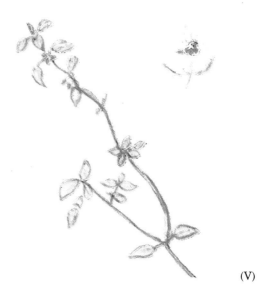

(V)

A perennial or much-branched herb, this shrub grows to a height of about 50cms. It has a long flowering period from June to September. The plant has small greyish-green leaves arranged in alternate pairs. The flowers are very pale mauve or whitish-yellow and are almost hidden by knotted bracts.

All **Marjorams** possess various quantities of a strong, aromatic oil. In Cyprus, in former times, the oil was collected for distillation and the village of Kambos was the centre of the industry. At the turn of the century the annual production from there was 1000 kilos of oil. Today a licence must be obtained from Department of Forestry to gather it on any scale.

The herb has been used as a flavouring herb since ancient times. It is easy to dry and retains its flavour well. In Cyprus the *"rigani"* is popular with grilled fish and meat, the bitterness countering the heavy oil sometimes used in cookery. It is the most delicately flavoured of all the **marjorams** with a fine, sweet scent, suited to salads and summer vegetables. Origano tea or *"tsai sapsishia"* is very popular in Cyprus which is thought to help ease the common cold and tonsilitis.

The oil has an antiseptic effect, is mildly tonic and digestive and is said to provoke menstruation. An infusion will settle the stomach and is helpful in cases of morning sickness. The oil or fresh leaves will soothe toothache and a pillow stuffed with the dried herb may help insomniacs. It is also thought beneficial as a massage for cases of rheumatism and aching limbs.

Marjoram was popular in times past as a sweetly scented disinfectant by strewing the leaves and stems around the house. The oil has also been used to polish wooden furniture.

The name "Origano" derives from the Greek words meaning "joy of the mountains" and in Greece the bridal pair used to be crowned with **marjoram.** It was also planted over graves to ensure a happy after-life.

Today, the villagers like to collect the stems for making brooms similar to the **Spiny Burnet.**

Location: Prolific growth on the hillsides of Paphos especially Tsada where, in the past, the villagers have earned a living collecting for the French perfumers.

Pancratium maritimum (Amaryllidiceaea)
SAND LILY, SEA PANCRATIUM
SEA DAFFODIL

Krinos tou Yialou

(A)

This large white 6-petalled flower is similar in appearance to a daffodil or a lily. It grows in groups with 3-12 flowers on one stem up to 25cms from a large bulb buried in the sand. Sadly the plant is becoming extinct due to careless feet tramping along the beaches.

Its blue-green strap-like leaves appear in June, then die down before the flowers suddenly emerge during July and August. At night the flower has a sweet and heavy aroma.

The seeds are black, large and covered with a spongy coating so they are able to float in the sea. In ancient times the plant was known as *"Dioscorides Pancratium"* famous for its use as an emetic.

Location: Sandy beaches. Once very common in the Famagusta and Ayia Napa areas but, due to tourism, its numbers are diminishing.

Eryngium maritimum (Umbelliferae)
SEA HOLLY   Lioprini tis Thalassa

(M)

This well-branched prickly perennial bears silver-grey leaves and numerous flower heads consisting of small metallic blue flowers surrounded by pale blue bracts. It grows to about 50cms high and is seen from June to August when the flowers mature in succession. The plant is very attractive to bees and butterflies.

The **Sea Holly** has a thick, fleshy rhizome and is well known for its aphrodisiac powers and as a cure for flatulence and other stomach complaints.

Even today, in the Paphos area, farmers still feed their sheep on the root as they firmly believe it will increase fertility.

Location: Along the coastal beaches particularly between Latchi and Limani in the Polis area, Yeroskipou, Ayia Napa and Famagusta.

Mentha pulegium (Labiatae)
PENNYROYAL   **Printziollos**

(V)

This highly aromatic herb grows to a height of 50-60cms. It has stems covered in white hairs from which oval-shaped leaves about 3-4cms long grow in pairs. The small lilac flowers form whorls in the axils of opposite bracts. The flowering period stretches from June until October.

Similar to other mints, the plant is rich in medicinal properties. Pliny recorded that more than 60 medicines are based on the scent of **Mint** and **Pennyroyal.** Its main use has been as an antiseptic and in infusions for treating mouth infections. **Pennyroyal** makes an effective tonic and in Cyprus the villagers enjoy eating the leaves as part of a salad. Chewing on the leaves has also been found useful as an effective breath freshener.

Location: Any wet soil mainly clay, along the sides of streams and rivers, especially Kythrea and Chrysochou area.

Crithmum maritimum (Umbelliferae)
ROCK SAMPHIRE
Kirtama

(M)

This much-branched perennial has a long flowering period from June to October. It is recognised by its greenish-yellow flower heads forming umbels at the end of stems 30-40cms long. Its aromatic leaves are thick and fleshy and deltoid in shape.

The villagers enjoy pickling the leaves and tender stems in vinegar. They are considered highly nutritous.

It has valuable medicinal properties and has been used as an effective purgative and in cases of indigestion. Due to the aromatic oil which the plant produces, **Rock Samphire** is still used today in perfumery.

Location: Along the coast amongst the rocks, especially in the Akamas area, Ayia Napa, Protaras and Cape Greco.

Dianthus strictus (Caryophyllaceae)
WILD PINK

Dianthus

This pretty little perennial has very fragile, pale pink flowers, one to a stem, which measure only 1-1½cms across. Each flower has 5 petals with a scalloped edge and dotted with a darker shade of pink. It has very tiny leaves which help to minimise the amount of moisture lost during the hot summer months. Its season therefore lasts right through to October. The **Wild Pink** was referred to in medieval times as a symbol of love.

Location: Lowlands in well-drained sandy soil and in rocky areas. There is a slightly larger endemic species found in the Troodos Mountains known as *"Dianthus strictus var. troodi"*.

(M)

Heliotrope europaeum (Boraginaceae)
HELIOTROPE

Heliotropia

This many branching annual which only grows to a height of approximately 40-50cms has oval, greyish-green leaves about 1.5-3cms long, covered on both sides with fine hairs. The white flowers with a yellowish base are very small, about 3-4mm across and are arranged in tight clusters forming a spike.

The plant is seen flowering on cultivated and wasteland from early June until September.

Location: Common all over Cyprus.

(M)

Echinops spinosissimus (Compositae)
VISCOUS GLOBE THISTLE   **Kamilangatho, Moskokavli**

(R)

This is one of the last thistles to appear in the year. This perennial is tall, reaching 3m in height. The leaves in the winter months form a large white-veined rosette close to the ground. In the early summer a large, branched and flowering stem grows up from the centre. It is covered with spines and brown, sticky hairs.

In July the flower appears as a shiny, globular head, about 7cms across, blue in colour.

Location: Common along the roadsides and wasteland.

(J)

Inula viscosa (Compositae)
INULA, ELECAMPE   **Konizos, Nerokollisia**

(J)

This bushy plant with its strong resinous smell has spear-shaped, sticky leaves, sometimes hairy and sometimes toothed. Each leaf stem is clustered with yellow flowers with orange coloured stamens and reaches a height of about 50cms.

The flowers bloom through the summer until September in the mountains and until November on the lower rocky slopes.

In Cyprus the villagers have found the plant useful to repel insects and fleas by hitting their mattresses with the fresh stems. Also they rub the shutters of their houses with the stems to deter the insects from entering.

The plant has been used medicinally also in the past, as a powder in the treatment of burns and as an infusion for enteritis and as a diuretic.

Location: Widespread in the lowlands and the highland.

ubus sanctus (Rosaceae)
RAMBLE, BLACKBERRY   Vatos, Vatsinia, Vramos

(M)

A perennial, this thorny climber is sometimes referred to as the Holy plant because it is stated in the Bible that God appeared to Moses in a flame of fire from the middle of the bush.

The plant blooms in July and August, propogated by seeds. It has a number of small white flowers with 5 petals, about 1cm long, numerous stamens with pink filaments and a yellowish centre. The small, edible reddish-black fruit is commonly known as the blackberry.

Dioscorides, referring to the **Bramble,** proclaims the considerable medical properties of the plant. Extracts from the leaves have been used externally to cure ulcers and injuries. An effective and pleasant tasting syrup can be made from the mature fruits to treat diarrhoea.

Location: Widespread along the roadsides and hedges from sea level to 1500m. Common in the Polis area.

Carlina pygmaea (Compositae)
DWARF CARLINE THISTLE   **Karlin**

(A

One of the last plants to be found before the winter, this attractive little thistle is seen in August through to October in coastal areas and in the lower hills. Sometimes it is difficult to spot being so small — it only grows to a height of about 12cms — and being located in the shelter of prickly bushes. It blends very easily into the background as the leaves and stems soon turn a little beige after propogation.

The plant is a biennial which forms a prickly rosette of leaves, soon dying away as the thistle flowers in the second year and leaving the flowering plant with stem leaves only. The flower heads are approximately 5cms in diameter in two colours, magenta and the more common gold.

This thistle is thought to be endemic to Cyprus. It is related to the larger **Golden Thistle** *"Carlina involucrata ssp. cyprica"* which can be seen all over Cyprus on uncultivated ground during the month of August.

Both the above thistles are popular with flower arrangers as they dry easily and keep their colour for many years.

Location: Widespread in the lower hills and along the coast among the rocks and stones.

Forest scene.

SHRUBS
and
TREES

As you wander along the floral path of Cyprus, you cannot fail to notice the number of magnificent trees and flowering shrubs which grace the island.

In Spring time a dazzling panorama of flowers and blossoming trees sets the whole countryside ablaze with colour.

The purple **jacarandas** and the pink and white **oleanders** are abundant along the roadsides. The **mimosa,** or **wattle,** as it is known in Cyprus, provides a brilliant golden splash against the turquoise blue of the Mediterranean.

Furthermore, a glorious scent from the **myrtle, almond, citrus** and other aromatic trees pervades the air. Both colour and fragrance are a delight to the senses.

The fruit blossom in the fertile valleys are especially wonderful to behold — **apple, pear, plum** and **cherry,** and how pleasant it is to wander through the orchards shortly after a gentle sprinkling of rain has enhanced their aroma!

The hinterland rises gradually to the mountains through vast areas of vines and forests. The scenery is magnificent and visitors to this part of Cyprus are always delighted to encounter such cool, fresh air, scented with the pungent smell of pine trees and wild herbs.

In former times, people used to come from all over the Mediterranean area to the Paphos district to worship Aphrodite passing through groves of flowering trees, myrtles and pomegranates, to rest a while in Yeroskipou, the Sacred Garden of Venus.

It is impossible to include all the magnificent trees of which Cyprus can boast in one chapter; I have selected those which are my personal favourites to describe for you and trust they will help you with identification during your wanderings. For any further information regarding trees, I would suggest you contact the Ministry of Agriculture and Natural Resources, the Forestry Department, who are always willing to help with enquiries.

Cherry
Blossom

(M)

Jacaranda
Blossom

(M)

Lemon
Tree

(R)

Orange Trees

(R)

Almond Blossoms

(M)

Bananas

(R)

mygdalus communis (Rosaceae)
LMOND TREE

Athasia

(R)

This popular tree is enjoyed not only for the delicious nuts it produces but also the beautiful, scented blossoms. It is a fairly small tree, 6-8 metres in height, being heavily laden with white and pale pink blossoms in January and February.

The **Almond Tree** has been cultivated in Cyprus since it was brought here from W. Asia.

The fruits of the tree are oval and pale green, 4cms long, splitting when ripe to reveal a pale brown stone within which is the edible kernal or seed. The seeds are eaten raw and used in cooking. They have a very high nutritional value. Almond oil is also widely used in the cosmetic industry.

At the monastery of Ayios Herakledios at Tamassos in the Nicosia district, the nuns are proud to produce *"glygo amygalo"* (preserved almonds) along with their scented rose james. Incidentally this monastery is also the best place in Cyprus to see water lilies.

Location: Lowlands and hills all over Cyprus.

Eriobotrya japonica (Rosaceae)
LOQUAT

Mespil

(J)

This tree originally brought to Cyprus from Japan has been cultivated for its juicy little fruits. It grows to a height of 8m with many branches covered in dark-grey hairs and large dark-green oval shaped leaves.

The whitish flowers grow in clusters and the oval fruits, 1-5-2cms wide are golden in colour. The tree shows its flowers in January and February.

The fruit, apart from being delicious to eat, is said to be good for "one's intestines".

Location: Lowland areas throughout Cyprus.

uniperus phoenicea (Cupressaceae)
'HOENICEAN JUNIPER   **Aoratos**

(M)

This evergreen shrub grows up to 10m high. The leaves are glandular about 1mm long and overlapped. The cones are cylindrical about 10-12mm in diameter and ripen in the second year to a dark reddish-brown colour.

Oil of **juniper** is distilled from the unripe berries and is used medicinally as a diuretic and in the treatment of cystitis and externally for dermatitis. The ripe berries are used for flavouring and in seasoning food.

Location: From sea level to about 350m on dry slopes, rocky ground and in Pine Forests. Very common in the Akamas and the Akrotiri areas.

Arbutus andrachne (Ericaceae)
STRAWBERRY
TREE   Antrouklia

This small evergreen shrub or tree can reach a height of 5m. It is easily recognisable by its smooth, red bark, large leathery dark-green leaves, which are grey underneath and egg-shaped, and by its clusters of creamy-white bell-shaped flowers which bloom between February and April.

The fruit of the tree are numerous, about 6mm in diameter, orange-red in colour, edible but insipid.

The leaves and bark have been used medicinally. An infusion was made from the leaves for diarrhoea, cystitis, and in respiratory cases.

Theophrastus wrote that women used the wood for parts of the loom.

Location: Maquis, rocky areas, forests.

(M)

Acacia dealbata (Leguminosae)
MIMOSA, SILVER WATTLE   Akakia

This attractive tree of Australian origin, has a smooth white trunk and long, leafy branches. It is characterised by the silvery down that covers its compound, paired leaves and young shoots. The beautiful yellow scented flowers grow in numerous, multi-branched clusters at the end of the branches. It can grow up to 30 metres in the wild but usually reaches 8-12 metres in cultivated areas.

It regenerates naturally and quickly by suckers and is often planted to stabilise the soil as well as for timber and ornament. The mimosa is very popular with flower arrangers.

Location: Sandy places along the coast, roadsides and waste places.

Lavendula stoechas (Labiatae)
FRENCH LAVENDER

Myrofora, Agriolevanda

This small compact shrub is similar in appearance to the cultivated lavender, having large purple flower heads and aromatic oils can be extracted from the plant in the same way. This plant grows to a height of between 30 and 60 centimetres and has small greyish green leaves covered in cottony hairs arranged close together and in opposite pairs. It blooms from February until June and then the plant appears to die only to shoot again later in the year.

The aromatic flower heads are used by the Orthodox church to decorate the Epitaph on Good Friday to signify the memory of Jesus Christ's burial. In Cyprus the villagers call the plant *"Lambri"* which means Easter.

In Greece and sometimes in Cyprus too the plant is referred to as *"Myrofora"* which means "Carriers of Perfume" after the women at Christ's tomb who bore perfumes and sweet smelling spices.

In medicine the **French Lavender** is used as an antiseptic in the treatment of wounds. Aromatic oils from the plant are also considered as therapeutic and relaxing if added to bath water.

(V)

Location: Common in the Troodos hills and well-drained rocky soils. Forest clearings. Akrotiri peninsular.

Cistus salvifolius (Cistaceae)
SAGE-LEAVED CISTUS,
SAGE-LEAVED ROCK ROSE, ROCK ROSE   **Psistarka**

(Y)

In Spring the Cyprus landscape is covered with various bushes of the **Cistus** species. The **Sage-leaved Cistus,** or more commonly called **Rock Rose,** has white flowers with orange centres and the leaves take their name from the herb called Sage which are aromatic when crushed. The plant is found in the lowlands during February to April and in the mountains in May.

There is a smaller variety of the white **Cistus** called *"Cistus Monspelienses"* which is also aromatic and sticky to touch. Its flowering period is April and May and can be seen growing from sea level to about 650 metres, mainly in the western part of the island. Another variety of **Cistus** growing in Cyprus is the *"Cistus incanus ssp. creticus",* also referred to as **Rock Rose** or *"Kounouklia"* in Cyprus.

It is often seen growing alongside the **Sage-leaves Rock Rose,** its purple scented flowers resembling roses and making a sharp contrast to the white variety. It has been recorded that in former times the plant was exported from Cyprus to Egypt and the Sudan and there used in medicine. It can be located in Cyprus on the lowlands and highlands on rocky ground between February and June.

All the **Cistus** species excude laudanum from its leaves, a brown gum used in medicine and in perfumery. This was collected by combing it out of the beards and hair of goats seen grazing amongst the plants.

aurus nobilus (Lauraceae)
AUREL, SWEET BAY   **Daphne**

(V)

This evergreen shrub with erect branches grows to about 8m high. It has very aromatic leaves, lance-shaped with wavy margins. The pale yellow, inconspicuous flowers grow in small clusters along the leaves, developing into shiny berries which ripen from green to black.

The **laurel** leaves which, in classical times, were worn in wreathes as a sign of victory, are today used in cookery as a flavouring. Both berries and leaves are said to be good for digestion. The oil from the plant is used in cosmetics and in the treatment of rheumatism.

Location: Common in all damp areas, flowering from February to April.

Sarcopoterium spinosum (Rosaceae)
SPINY BURNET, THORNY BURNET

Maz

This plant takes the form of a prickly bush about 0.5m high from May round to February when many of the villagers use the stiff, matted branches as brooms or in making fires. In early Spring, green leaves start to appear, followed by clusters of male and female flowers; the female ones recognisable by their reddish-purple feathery stamens whilst the yellow flowers, with their long stamens, are male.

Tight bundles of fruit soon appear about 5 millimetres in diameter which turn a brownish-red as they develop.

(M)

The fruits have been used throughout the ages, crushed and made into a tonic or as a diuretic.

Location: Widespread from sea level to approximately 1200m high; wastelands and open forest areas.

Phagnalon graeca (Compositae)
GRECIAN FLEABANE

The name **"Fleabane"** has been applied to this and several related plants which were dried and placed in beds to drive fleas away. It is a small perennial shrub up to 30cms high, often seen on cliffs and in stony areas.

Towards the end of January the yellow flower heads open, surrounded by chocolate coloured scales and, if the flowers are picked before they are fully open, they make an attractive contribution towards dried arrangements at home, and will last for at least a year.

Location: Coastal areas on cliffsides and rocky ledges.

(Y)

Calycotome villosa (Papilionaceae)
PRICKLY BROOM

Raski

(M)

This thorny shrub, very common to Cyprus, blooms from March to April with clusters of bright yellow flowers shaped like peas. The flowers are heavily scented and contain a trip mechanism which sprays any bees alighting on them. In Spring the leaves wither and fall and by the summer the branches have dried and turned grey. The side shoots which bore the flowers turn black and harden into sharp thorns, hence its name. The whole plant is covered with fine grey hairs and grows to a height of about 1-2m.

Another variety of **Broom** grows in Cyprus, the *"Genista sphacelata"* which has smaller flowers, simple leaves and a 2-lipped calyx. It appears after the *"Calycotome villosa"* but is more widespread, appearing in great abundance on all the hillsides. A sub-species "Genista sphacelata var. crudelis" grows high on Troodos forming a striking yellow carpet.

From April to August a variety called **Spanish Broom** *(Spartium junceum)* is quite prolific along the roadsides. This plant is easily recognisable because of its tall, smooth, spineless and almost leafless stems.

The large attractive flowers are a strong yellow colour and grow in loose clusters at the end of stems.

It is said that if shepherds feed their sheep and goats on this plant they will be resistant to snake bites.

Location: Broom is found all over Cyprus in rocky areas especially on hillsides.

(J)

PRICKLY BROOM

We welcome the fragrance in Summer,
That bee-triggered perfume of Broom:
Beware of the same shrub in Winter,
Its' thorns demand plenty of room!

Cupressus sempervirens (Cupressaceae)
FUNERAL CYPRESS
Kyparissi

This handsome tall tree grows to a height of between 15-30m. The crown appears either narrow and columnar, tapering to a pointed tip, or pyramid-shaped with spreading level branches. The bark is brownish-grey with shallow, spiralled ridges. The small leaves are dark green, scale-like and triangular, 1mm long, arranged in overlapping rows that completely cover the twigs.

It flowers between March and May, forming male and female cones. The male cones are green and egg-shaped, 3mm long. The female cones are 4 x 3cms, green and globular, becoming dark reddish-brown and finally a dull grey.

Cypress cones have been used medicinally since ancient times, especially in the treatment of anaemia and glandular fever.

The timber is very strong, durable and fragrant. Being resistant to decay, it has been used in the past for carving furniture and staking vine crops.

The **Cypress** has long been revered by the islanders and many believe that Cyprus has been named after it.

(M)

Location: Common throughout Cyprus.

Ferula communis (Umbelliferae)
GIANT FENNEL   **Anarthrika**

(M)

This perennial is very prolific during March and April.

It has green leaves with tiny yellow flowers forming an umbrella-shaped head or umbel. It is very tall growing to a height of about 3 metres.

Another plant of this species *"Foeniculum vulgare"* known in Cyprus as *'Marathos',* can be seen growing along the roadsides between April and September. This **Yellow Fennel** is shorter than the **Giant Fennel,** growing to about 2m and has brighter yellow flowers.

Both the stems and leaves, which smell of aniseed, are cut when green and often used in cookery e.g. in soup and casseroles and is particularly used to flavour red mullet *(Barbouni* in Greek). There are records of the use of Fennel in cooking dating back to Ancient Times.

Hippocrates and Dioscorides recommended it to wet nurses to activate the secretion of milk, as well as to persons threatened by blindness. The Chinese and Hindus used **Fennel** to neutralise snake bites and scorpion stings; and sorcerers believed that sprigs of **Fennel** hung from the rafters would drive out evil spirits and the seeds inserted into keyholes would bar the way to ghosts.

In medicine, dried **Fennel** seeds have been prescribed in the past for stomach disorders, loss of appetite, inflammation of the mucus, to strengthen the nerves and to combat chronic headaches and migraines. A decoction of **Fennel** root is said to stimulate the appetite.

In Cyprus, fishermen use the thick dry stems of **Fennel** after the plants have died during the summer to make little stools for their boats and for floating upturned on the sea at night, with a lamp inside, to mark the position of their nets. They also cut up the stems to use as corks for their water carriers.

Location: Fields and roadsides in abundance all over Cyprus.

Platanus orientalus (Platanaceae)

ORIENTAL PLANE   **Platanos**

This large tree, reaching about 30m has a straight trunk and massive yellowish-green bark.

Its leaves are about 18cms long by 8cm wide with 5-7 lobes.

Borne on yellowish stalks 5cms long, the leaves turn from pale orange-brown to yellow green and finally to pale bronze purple.

Location: Wet localities and river valleys.

Pinus brutia (Pinaceae)
ALEPPO PINE   **Agriopevko**

(M)

This species of **pine** is the most predominant on the island, covering large areas from sea level to 1600m. The tree has bright green needle-shaped leaves, 6-10cms long, and grows to a height of approximately 10-20m, branching from the base.

The cones are bright reddish-brown, pointed and egg-shaped, and they remain on the tree for several years. The tree is known to be very drought-resistant and, according to Theophrastus, was an important timber tree and used by the Ancient Greeks in ship and house-building. It is tapped for its resin and is an important tree fuel.

Location: Limestone hills near the sea, rocky ground to 1600m.

unica granatum (Punicaceae)

POMEGRANATE

Rodia

(M)

This small deciduous tree growing to a height of about 5-6m originally came from S.W. Asia. Legend has it that Aphrodite first planted it on Cyprus.

Its leaves are slender and shiny, bright green in colour, and 3-7cms long. The plant is admired for its large orange-red blooms, about 3-4cms across. The sepals are united in a tube from which 4 crumpled petals and many stamens emerge. The fruit is a large berry 5-8cms across with a brownish-red leathery stem, containing numerous seeds surrounded by a pinkish pulp.

The fruit is eaten raw and its juice can be drunk fresh or made into wine; the seeds are used in jams and syrups. The bark, rind and roots of the tree were formerly used medicinally especially as a worm powder. The juice is still given to patients suffering from kidney disease.

The **pomegranate** plant is recognised as a symbol of fertility and, in some Cypriot villages, even today, a **pomegranate** is thrown on the ground at the entrance to their new home in order that it will split and release the many seeds, encouraging fertility.

Location: Widespread throughout Cyprus usually as a hedge plant. It flowers between April and June.

Riccinus communis (Euphorbiaceae)
CASTER OIL TREE

Kourtounia

This small tree has an erect, branched stem, reaching 4-5m in height. It is easily recognised by its large reddish-brown leaves cut into 5-9 lance shaped lobes, and reddish flowers growing in spikes in spherical clusters. It flowers from April to May.

Caster Oil has been used medicinally for many years as a purgative and an emollient.

Location: Any wasteland.

(M)

Pinus negra (Pinaceae)
PINE TREE

Mantopefkos

(R)

This popular tree, a hardy evergreen, reaches a height of 15-18m. It has an irregular crown with dark brown, spreading branches. The scaly bark is black-brown to dark grey and coarsely ridged. The leaves are dark green to black needles, curved and sharply pointed, usually in pairs, 5-12cms long, 1-2mm wide. The tree flowers from April to May, forming male and female cones. The male cones appear in clusters, yellowish brown in colour. The female cones are solitary or in clusters 5-8cms long.

The resin, together with infusions made from the leaves, have often been used as a diuretic and antiseptic.

Location: Troodos Mountains above 1200m. Grows along with the Junipe tree at Chionistra.

Nerium oleander (Apocynaceae)
OLEANDER　　　　　　　　　Arodaphne or Rododaphne

This attractive shrub is seen growing in Cyprus in gravelly places, damp ravines and along water edges. It is a tall, strong plant up to 4m high with stiff branches and long, pointed, leathery leaves, greyish-green in colour. The fairly large flowers grow in clusters at the end of stems, usually bright pink in colour sometimes red or white. These beautiful, almond scented flowers belie its poisonous nature. The whole plant exudes a white, milky juice which is highly toxic even though it was suggested in Ancient Greece that "the addition of a root of **Oleander** to wine would modify the temper". About 2000 years ago, Dioscorides, the famous Greek physician, said that "while the tree was poisonous it also yielded an effective medicine". When taken with wine he said that it was "wholesome for men against the bites of animals, especially if mixed with Rue, but when the smaller animals, like goats and sheep drink of this, they die". The plant was said to have a bad effect on dogs, asses and most 4-legged animals.

In India it is known as the "horse killer" and is used as a funeral plant in both Hindu and Christian religions. It is further recorded that during the Peninsular War some French soldiers used **Oleander** wood as skewers for meats and of the 12 who ate the meat, 7 died and the rest were seriously ill. It is obviously a plant to be handled very carefully. In Cyprus it is used as a rat poison.

Location: Along roadsides, damp ravines, along water edges throughout the summer months.

Eucalyptus torquata (Myrtaceae)
EUCALYPTUS TREE, GUM TREE   Efkalyptos

(M)

These evergreen trees only occur naturally in Australia and Tasmania. It is recorded that the **Eucalyptus** was brought to Cyprus by the British during the early years of their rule, and now more than 70 different species have been recorded on the island.

Eucalyptus trees are fast growers and can reach a height of 10 metres if left unpruned. The form of a mature tree is characteristic, a sparsely-branched tree of a cream colour with a rough, dark brown bark. This bark is usually shed after four or five years to expose the pale cream bark underneath. This darkens after a while which causes a striking mottled effect.

The branches are covered with pendulous sickle-shaped leaves which are very aromatic and highly regarded medicinally for their antibiotic and antiseptic qualities. **Eucalyptus** oil is frequently used to make inhalants as an effective cure for catarrh, sinusitis, bronchitis and asthma.

Prolific flowering usually occurs when the trees are from 4-6 years old. In the *"Eucalyptus torquata"* species, 5-9 red flowers occur in umbels from the leaf axils in early summer. They have numerous stamens and bright red filaments about 1cm long.

Eucalyptus foliage is excellent for flower arrangements. Cut in winter, it will live for several weeks and the young summer growths will last several days if the stems are scalded for about 15 seconds after cutting.

Location: Different species seen all over the island — the partial shade cast by **Eucalyptus** trees is excellent for rhododendrons and other woodland shrubs. The *"Eucalyptus torquata"* is cultivated in parks and gardens in the Nicosia area.

Myrtus communis (Myrtaceae)
COMMON MYRTLE

Mersini

This dense green shrub with brown stems and balsam-like leaves grows to a height of approximately 1.3m. Its flowers are similar in appearance to the caper flowers except that it has 5 instead of 4 white petals and its numerous stamens are tipped with yellow. It is very sweet-scented and bears flowers from May to September when the fruits appear as round black berries, edible and thought to have medicinal properties.

An aromatic oil is produced from its shiny, green leaves seen growing in pairs, and from the flowers and the bark of the shrub.(M) *"Myrtus"* is the Greek word for perfume. The oil is also used as an antiseptic and a nasal decongestant. It is also used in cosmetics, added to bath water as a relaxant and is reputed to be beneficial to the skin.

Before talcum powder was invented to Cyprus the leaves were finely ground and used as powder.

The **Common Myrtle** is a shrub steeped in legend. One amusing anecdote is that a girl will not succeed in rooting cuttings of the **Myrtle** if she is destined to be an old maid. In ancient Greece the **Myrtle** had been used in bridal bouquets but the bride was always warned not to plant the sprigs. The **Myrtle** has always been considered a symbol of love and peace and happy marriage, and devoted to Aphrodite, the Goddess of love and beauty who in legend was born from the foam of the sea along the southern shore of Cyprus. In former times the branches were used to make wreaths for crowning heroes, and today they are still used in the making of wreaths and for laying in the church during Easter.

Location: Rocky slopes, river banks and by streams in the Troodos and Pendataktylos areas: Maquis-evergreen thickets.

Lonicera etrusca (Caprifoliaceae)
HONEYSUCKLE

Ayioklima, Pontitzia

(M)

This climbing shrub of up to 3m high can be seen over hedgerows and sprawling along rough ground. The dark green leaves, 4-8cms long and 2-4cms wide are stalkless and grow in pairs. The cream flowers are arranged in clusters, each cluster having 4-12 flowers.

They are trumpet-shaped with protruding stamens about 2cms long. The fruit appears as a tight head of red berries about 1cm across. The honeysuckle flowers between May and July.

The bark of this **Honeysuckle** is found to have diuretic qualities and, in Cyprus, it has been used in the past as an emetic to treat poisoning from left-over food cooked in copper saucepans.

Location: Particularly prolific in areas between 300 and 1500 metres in the highlands and forest areas especially in the area of the Kykko Monastery; Stavros tis Psokas.

Olea europaea (Oleaceae)
OLIVE TREE

Elaia

(J)

This tree, sacred to Greece, has been widely cultivated in the Mediterranean area for fruit since ancient times. It grows wild in dry, rocky places reaching a height of 15m. In Paphos it grows wild but is also under supervision as the fruit and oil are consumed locally and constitute an essential part of the Cypriot diet.

The tree is easily recognised by its spreading crown supported on twisted gnarled bark, silvery grey in colour. The wood, which is very hard, is used for carving cabinetwork, fuel and charcoal.

The flowers are small and white, growing in dense clusters in the axils of the leaves.

The fruit is egg-shaped 2-3.5 cms long, containing a single large seed, which ripens from green to black.

Olive oil, apart from being a high quality cooking oil, is used medicinally in ointments and in making soap.

Location: The lowlands and hills all over Cyprus.

Capparis spinosa (Capparidaceae)
CAPER

Kapparka or Kappari

The sweet scented flowers of this plant bloom from late May until August. They only open after sunset when they attract the moths and bees before the flowers droop and shrivel up in the strong daylight. The plant grows as a spiny, much branched shrub about 1.5m high, dark blue-green leaves and prickly spines. The flowers have 4 large, white petals and 4 mauvish sepals. From the centre emerge a number of long stamens tinged with purple. The fruit is an oblong berry about 5cms long containing many seeds.

It is a custom in Cyprus to collect the unopened flower buds, dry them in the hot sun, pickle them and sometimes sell them as *"Koutrouvi"* a well-known appetiser. The young shoots and immature fruits are also pickled as *"Kapari",* and served in salads.

The **Caper** plant is also well known for its medicinal properties. The buds and roots have been used as an antiseptic and diuretic. It is also used as a tonic to help the common cold and in the treatment of eye infections.

Location: Seen all over Cyprus in rocky places, ancient ruins and wasteland.

Vitex agnus castus (Verbenaceae)
MONKS PEPPER TREE, CHASTE TREE

Agnia, Lygaria

This perennial shrub is known in Cyprus as *"Ligaria"* or *"Ligia"*, so called because of its malleable branches which the villagers use for making baskets and wicker ware.

It is also referred to as *"Agnia"* from the Greek *"Agnos"* meaning pure or chaste. Dioscorides said that the seeds of this plant have the power to subdue the natural inclination between the two sexes, hence **"Monk's Pepper"**.

The plant is quite tall, growing to a height of approximately two to three metres. It blooms throughout the summer with a small cluster of flowers at the end of each stem, in a violet blue shade.

(M)

Location: Sandy coastal areas, river sides, mainly in the lowland areas.

Rhus coriaria (Anacardiaceae)
SUMACH

Soumakia

Recognised by its hairy shoots, this shrub is almost evergreen, retaining at least a few leaves for most of the winter. It grows to a height of about 2.5 metres.

Its leaves are thick and velvety deep green with 4-8 toothed leaflets which, in the Autumn, turn a greenish-red. Its small flowers are greenish packed into dense, erect spikes. The fruits are purplish-brown and hairy, currant-sized in dense clusters.

The dry fruits are used in Cyprus as a spice, usually included in *"Souvlakia"*, a traditional dish. The sumach is also well reputed for its medicinal qualities for diarrhoea, intestinal problems and dermatitis. The plant is probably more well-known for the tan its leaves produce for the leather industry, and as a natural dye. Many tons of **Sumach** leaves are collected in Cyprus and exported abroad for processing.

Location: Rocky roadsides, mountainous areas. Common around Pitsilia.

Agave Americana (Amaryllidaceae)
AMERICAN ALOE, CENTURY PLANT   Aloe athanatos

(M)

This gigantic plant begins its life similar to a cactus with tough, pointed leaves growing across the ground to about 4 metres in diameter. After approximately 10 years a huge, branched flowering spike appears from the centre of the rosette in May which will have grown to a height of about 6-8 metres by June. In July numerous yellow flowers open and then, after they die, the whole plant also dies.

The plant is known as the **American Aloe** because it is thought to have been introduced to Cyprus from South America several hundred years ago.

Location: Rocky, dry and sandy ground.

eratonia siliqua (Leguminosae)

AROB TREE

Charoupia, Teratsomelo

(M)

This large tree has a thick, dark brown trunk and long, leathery leaves. It reaches a height of about 6-10m.

The greenish flowers are very small, growing in a spike, and the fruit are contained in a large, also leathery, pod 10-25cms long. These pods are rich in sugary pulp which the villagers store to make *"Charoupomelo"* or *"Teratsomelo"* (Carob Tree honey).

About 300,000 kilos of carobs are grown in Cyprus today, but, in fact, since the birth of Christ they have had utmost significance. They were said to be the main source of food for John the Baptist when he was in the wilderness. As a consequence the pods are sometimes referred to as "St. John's Bread". The trees have also been referred to as the "Black Gold of Cyprus".

The villagers produce a delicacy from the carob syrup called *"Pastelli"*, a thick, golden sweet which, when cold, is cut into fingers.

The seed inside the pod is also used in cosmetics. It was also the original carat which goldsmiths used to measure gold. Another common use for the pods here in Cyprus is as animal fodder.

Location: Dry and rocky ground all over Cyprus.

Ficus carica (Moraceae)
FIG

Syki

This very popular tree in Cyprus has a spreading crown with stout, knobbly, unswept branches and reaches a height of 5m. Its bark is smooth and metallic grey, finely patterned in a darker grey. The large leaves are thick, dark green with 3-5 lobes and very rough with hairs above and beneath. The flowers are tiny, enclosed in the fleshy-pear shaped fig which has a small hole at the top through which pollinating insects enter. The green fruit becomes violet or black when ripe. Half ripe figs are considered to be poisonous. The tree is seen to flower between August and November.

The leaves and stem exude a milky juice when cut which can be used as an effective treatment for boils, warts and insect bites.

The fruit is eaten fresh or dried and has strong laxative properties.

The fig was very important in Biblical times and, according to Theophrastus, fig wood is easily bent and it was thus useful for making theatre seats, hoops, garlands and ornaments.

Location: Widespread on the island.

(M

Cedrus libani ssp. brevifolia (Pinaceae)

CEDAR OF LEBANON

Kethros

(A)

There are 30,000 of these trees on the island, all protected by law. This species of **Cedar** is endemic to Cyprus. It is a native of the Lebanese mountains, Syria and S.E. Turkey.

Its crown is conical becoming flat-topped with wide spreading level branches. Its leaves are composed of dark green needles, growing in tufts of 10-12 on short spurs.

The mature female cones are 7-12cms long. The male cones are only 3-5cms long.

Location: The Cedar Valley near Stavros tis Psokas.

THE CYPRUS LANDSCAPE

Cyprus has a truly magnificent landscape. Every area has its own special appeal — a traveller's paradise. It is the third largest island in the Mediterranean, and the main physical characteristics of its 3572 square miles are the large Central Plain, The Mesaoria, with its mountain ranges of Pendataktylos to the north and Troodos to the south, and a varied coastline of rocks, cliffs and abundant beaches.

There are three main types of vegetation apparent as one ascends from sea-level to the Troodos Mountains:— the Garigue or dry lowlands, the Maquis, a large area of the island where the forest has been destroyed by fire or excessive grazing, or where the rainfall cannot support trees, and the forest area.

The hills and mountain regions above 1000 to 1200m are forested with conifers. The alpine area above 1900-1950m is mainly shrubland. The forest above 1500m is dominated by the **Troodos Pine** *(Pinus negra)* or *"Mantopefkos"* as it's known locally.

At 1300-1400m in the famous Cedar Valley at Stavros tis Psokas, one can see a forest of the Cyprus **Cedar** *(Cedrus libani),* and below this the **Aleppo Pine** *(Pinus Brutia)* or *"Agriopefkos"* in Greek, dominates. Up to 1800m you can see evergreen bushes of the **Golden Oak** *(Quercus infectoria),* which is endemic to Cyprus. Oak trees were once common on the island. The fact that many Cypriot villages have names related to *'Dhrys',* the Greek name for Oak tree, indicates that trees were once prevalent here.

History tells us that in former times vast areas of Cyprus were covered with forests, hence its reputation as the "Green Island of the Mediterranean". The wood was used for the building of the fleets of the Eastern Mediterranean countries. Sheep and goat grazing, fires and neglect destroyed most of the trees. One of the first things the British administration did in 1878 after Turkish occupation, was to re-establish part of the forest and in 1880 the Forestry Department was established which has followed a programme of afforestation and conservation ever since.

On the drive towards Larnaca, a green forest of healthy young trees decorates a hillside devoid of vegetation, making a sharp contrast to the white, chalky landscape. Today, the forest land now covers some 18% of the island.

In the valleys some familiar deciduous trees are growing in abundance — trees such as the **Oriental Plane** *(Platanus orientalis),* and the **Maple** *(Acer obtusifolium).*

olis Coast (M)   *Foothills of Troodos* (M)

In the Maquis below the forest's many shrubs are dominant, such as the **Cistus** *(cistus incanus ssp. creticus),* **Broom** *(calycotome villosa)* and **Oleander** *(Nerium oleander)* intermingling between the **Carob tree** *(Ceratonia siliqua),* the **Olive tree** *(Olea europea),* the **Sumach** *(Rhus coriaria)* and the **Juniper** *(Juniperus phoenicea).*

The third type of vegetation the "Garigue" is dominated by low shrubs less than 1m high, such as **Spiny Burnet** *(sarcopoterium spinosum)* and **Grecian Fleabane** *(Phagnalon graeca)* with many well-known herbs growing in profusion between the scattered bushes — thyme, sage and so on.

If you wish to visit the Forestry area to see some of these beautiful trees, it is possible to stay at the Stavros Forestry Station by booking in advance. The Cyprus Tourist Office publishes annually a list of places to stay in the Troodos mountains, as well as other resorts on the island.

Dhiarizos Valley (R)   *Curium Beach* (M)

It is a very useful leaflet, covering accommodation from the most sophisticated hotel to the more economical establishment. Basic accommodation is available at 5 of the island's monasteries. Bedding, towels and soap are provided usually and meals can be obtained locally.

One of the best ways to see areas of the countryside not troubled by too many tourists is to put on a pair of strong shoes, take a rucksack containing a few essentials, a good walking guide and set off for a ramble. There are several very concise maps and guides produced by the tourist office with carefully planned and suggested walks. The best sign-posted walks are in the Central Troodos mountain region around Platres and Troodos itself. The focal point is Mount Olympus and within a 15-mile radius there is a wide choice for ramblers.

There are some wonderful walks along the coast around the Ayia Napa, Cape Greco area in the southeast of the island; interesting walks from Larnaca to the Stavrovouni Monastery and others further to the south-east; from Limassol the Troodos mountains are only half an hour away by car, and in the northwest of the island, just an hour's drive from Paphos are the spectacular and unspoiled hills and valleys of the Akamas peninsular.

A very useful guide for getting around the countryside has been produced by "Sunflower Books". It is called "Landscapes of Cyprus" and is divided into three sections; the first for motorists, the second one for picnickers and the third for walkers, listing suggested walks covering 190 kilometres.

If you want to take a picnic on your explorations, the Cyprus Tourist Office and the Forestry Department have established around 20 excellent sites for picnicking. A leaflet about these sites is available from the Tourist Information Office.

Tragically, since the Turkish invasion of 1974, a line physically divides the island into two and it is not possible to travel freely between the two sectors except for a 24 hour period (through the Ledra checkpoint in Nicosia). The line which divides them runs west from Old Famagusta through Nicosia to the Bay of Morphou, reserving the fertile plain Mesaoria Plain and coastal mountains to the Turks, and leaving the Troodos Mountains and southern cities of Limassol, Larnaca and Paphos to the Greeks.

Moutoulas Village (R)   *Akamas Peninsula* (R)

For a very concise and fully illustrated travel guide of Cyprus, containing many subjects ranging from history, geography and culture, I would recommend "Explore Cyprus" by Renos Lavithis, which you will find covers the needs of every modern traveller to Cyprus.

For readers wishing to participate in special excursions relating to bird-watching, shepherd's haunts, and discovering the flora, I can strongly recommend contacting EXALT (Excursion Alternatives), a Paphos-based agency. This company escorts small groups to the more unusually spectacular areas of the Cyprus landscape.

Almond Trees (R)   *Paphos Forest* (R)

Kalopanayiotis Dam

CTO

Akamas - Island

CTO

Mountains near Makheras Monastery (R)

Vines and Almond Tree Fields (M)

Section Five

OTHER WILDLIFE

An Introduction to other Wildlife

I feel that I could not conclude this book without drawing your attention to some of the other extraordinarily beautiful wildlife which prevails on the island of Cyprus. After all, the balance of nature requires certain inter-dependencies; flowers need the birds to dispel their seeds, the birds need insects to survive and the butterflies need certain plants to feed upon.

I have, therefore, made a personal selection of my favourite birds, butterflies, reptiles and mammals, not only to add interest to this book but, perhaps, to encourage my readers to learn more about the unique natural history of Cyprus.

I have only summarised these subjects but there are some extremely informative books available in most of the major bookshops on the island e.g.

- Birds of Cyprus and Migrants
  of the Middle East
  by David and Mary Bannerman.
- Common Birds of Cyprus by J.M.E. Took.
- Butterflies of Cyprus by R. Parker,
  Entomologist Gazette, Vol. 34, March 1983.
- Birds of Europe and Britain by Collins.
- Nature of Cyprus by C. Georgiades.

OUR FEATHERED FRIENDS

As you stroll along the nature trails in Cyprus take a little time to stop, listen and look at the birds which are flying overhead or nestling in a tree. Acquaintance with birds provides a fuller and richer life for most individuals.

Art and literature from the beginning of human history have been exemplified with bird lore, and the names of many birds can be traced back to Greek legends.

Those who love and respect birds will never lack for company outdoors. Cyprus is a unique place for bird observation; Chrysochou Bay near Paphos is of particular importance. Bird watching as a hobby creates joy and excitement for there is always a new bird to spot and hear. On the island there are endless opportunities to spot a new bird in flight or, for some species like the Warbler, song is the best method of identification.

One of the most popular feathery visitors to Cyprus is the **"Olivaceous Warbler** *(Hippolais pallida),* Greek *"Spinnos",* who like to nestle in the **Olive** trees to breed. It lays 5 eggs and hops continuously from one branch to another noisily searching for food. The villagers have their own name for this slender brown bird "The *Trinitoura"* or chatterbox, a name sometimes given also to the village gossip.

Another member of the Warbler family, the "Sylviidae" is the **Reed Warbler** *(Acrocephalus scirpaceus),* Greek *"Spinnos",* who breeds in the lake of Akrotiri, nesting in the reeds. It is also small and slender and medium brown in colour.

A bird endemic to Cyprus is the very small **Cyprus Warbler** *(Sylvia melanothorax)* Greek *"Spinnos",* about 14cms long. This bird is very common in Cyprus and is referred to as the National bird. It is black in colour, the male being darker than the female. Its main characteristic, however, is the red ring round the eyes and its red iris. The **Cyprus Warbler** nests in bushes and lays 3-5 eggs.

Another member of the *"Sylviidae"* family, but with a much sweeter song, is the **Nightingale** *(Luscinia megarhynchos)* Greek *"Anthoni"*. It is a small brown bird with a rust coloured tail and can usually only be seen in the Troodos Mountains where it goes to breed. It likes to build its nest so low that sometimes the nest can be seen on the ground. Although it sings with full throaty notes even during the day, it is mostly heard at night under a bright moon. The islanders revere this bird and, unlike most other birds, its numbers are fortunately increasing.

Due to its geographical location, Cyprus has always been on the route followed by most of Europe's migratory birds as they travel to Africa in the Autumn and back to Europe in the Spring. Other factors which attribute to the island's popularity is the warm climate and the abundance of insects.

Also included among our feathered visitors are the **Swallows Herons, Gulls, Cranes, Pelicans** and **Geese.** Birds such as **Flamingoes, Moorhens, Coots** and birds of prey like to spend their winter on Cyprus, mainly due to its size and a great variety of habitats.

A recent estimate showed that there are 357 bird species in Cyprus, both migratory and permanent. The permanent residents are about 50 and, of the 307 specics which migrate through Cyprus, 27 breed regularly on the island.

Some of the birds which stop as they return from Africa to spend the summer here are the **Nightingales, Turtle Doves** and **Swallows.**

The **Swallows** (Hirundo rustica) Greek *"Helidonia",* build nests of mud and twigs all over Cyprus along the coast and on the plains, and in the Troodos Mountains. Fortunately, the **Swallow** is regarded in Cyprus as a holy bird so their nests are left undisturbed and it can safely lay 3-6 eggs twice and sometimes three times a year in the same nest. A small, friendly bird, it has dark blue upper parts, a dark red face and a blue breast. Underneath it is white with a pink breast.

The **Red-Rumped Swallow** *(Hirundo daurica)* Greek *"Helidono to portokalohroun",* is recognisable from the **Swallow** by its orange rump. It seems to favour building its nest on bridges and lays 3-5 white eggs.

Bee Eater

Swallow

Hooper

Roller

(V)

The **Swallows** are the first of our feathered friends to arrive on the island with the **Swifts** and the **House Martins,** usually in mid-February.

The **Black Swift** *(Capus apus), Greek "Petrohelidoni",* does not make any nests but likes to seek out holes in the roofs of houses where it will lay 2 or 3 eggs. Unusually, mating occurs in mid-air. The **Swift** will very often fly very high during the day and will even sleep in the sky. After the sun sets, it will descend to the ground very slowly, waking up as it approaches the ground before entering its hole again. When thirsty, the **Swift** can be observed swooping from a great height to scoop up water from rivers, dams and water tanks. It is a small bird that looks all black with very long crescent-shaped wings and a short forked tail. You can recognise it from the **Swallow** and the **House Martin** because it has no white underneath.

A larger species of the **Swift,** the **Pallid Swift** *(Apus pallidus)* Greek *"Petrohelidoni",* which is a lighter colour, greyish-brown, can only be seen in the Troodos Mountains. An even bigger bird of the species, the **Alpine Swift** *(Apus melba)* Greek *"Petrohelidoni",* seeks out holes in craggy mountain and rock surfaces to lay its eggs.

The **House Martin** *(Delichon urbica),* Greek *"Helidoni to parthalon"* builds its nest all over the island, including the tops of mountains. This bird is smaller than the **Swallow** and has a short forked tail. Its colouring is dark blue on the upper side with a face, underparts and rump in white. It lays 4-6 white eggs.

Later in the Spring, the elegant **Turtle Dove** *(streptopelia turtur)* arrives in Cyprus. This slender bird is recognised by its unusual colouring; a light reddish-brown back covered with black spots, a black tail with white edges, a grey head with pink underparts and a patch of black and white stripes on each side of the neck. It can be seen at all altitudes, and its nest consists of a delicate arrangement of twigs in trees or bushes. It lays 2 white eggs.

A bird which breeds regularly on the island is the magnificent **Eleonora's Falcon** *(Falco eleonorae)* Greek *"Falconi tis Eleonoras"* and, at one time, as many as 100 pairs were sighted between Akrotiri and Venus Rocks near Paphos. Legend has it that the bird takes its name from Eleonora, wife of Peter the First, who ruled in Cyprus during the Middle Ages. According to the Chronicle of Machairas, many of the kings and princes as well as Queen Eleonora, used the falcon for amusement and hunting. When people saw the bird in flight they referred to it as **"Eleonora's falcon"**. The bird usually arrives here in April but does not breed until the Autumn, laying 2 to 3 eggs in depressions in the high, rocky ledges of sea cliffs. Its plumage varies from pale brown to almost black. It feeds on the small birds which migrate here during Spring and Autumn.

A very high proportion of our feathered friends favour the two Salt Lakes as a wintering place. Two streams of birds converge on Akrotiri. One comes from Central Europe, the Balkans and Scandinavia via the Bosphorus; the second from Russia and Siberia via the Caspian Sea and the Black Sea. Cyprus is their last stepping stone before flying to Egypt and down the Nile Valley to Ethiopia and the great lakes of Central Africa. Recent estimates have shown that the total number of birds passing through Cyprus in Autumn is more than 150 million of many different species, with a smaller number returning in the Spring.

The most famous winter visitor to the Lakes is the **Greater Flamingo** *(Phoenicopterus ruber)* Greek *'Flamingos'*. The first **Flamingoes,** mainly adults, arrive in November and, after a short stay, migrate further to the south. During December the numbers increase with many juvenile birds also arriving.

Until March the young birds gather in schools protected by the adult birds. In April the first birds start to leave and by mid-July, all the birds have left. When young, the **Flamingo's** plumage is brown and by June of their first year, it begins to turn pink. It likes to feed on the special type of shrimp, the **Brine Shrimp** *(Artemia salini)* produced in the Salt Lakes. Aquatic birds are protected by law in Cyprus and the Akrotiri Salt Lake is a favourite stopping place with these birds.

Some of the species found there are the **Coot** *(Fulica atra)* Greek *"Karapattas"*, a medium sized black bird with a little white on the upper wing; the **Little Grebe** *(Podiceps ruficollis)* Greek *"Voutiktis"*, a tubby, brown bird with no tail, short neck and short pointed bill, and the **Black-Winged Stilt** *(Himantopus himantopus)* Greek *"Kalamokannas"*, a medium sized black and white bird with extremely long bright pink legs.

Another aquatic bird which seems to favour the Larnaca Salt Lake is the **Kentish Plover** *(charadrius alexandrinus)* Greek *"Ploumouthi"*, a small, plump light greyish-brown bird with white underneath.

My personal favourite of our feathered visitors is the very attractive, brightly-coloured **Bee-Eater** *(Merops apiaster)* Greek *"Melisofagos"*, who used to make its nests in the holes of river banks but now does so only rarely. Its blue breast, yellow throat and rich red-brown upper parts are very recognisable. Its long wings are yellow, brown and blue and the long centre of the tail is very conspicuous. You can often see it perched on telephone wires and bare branches when its long curved bill and tail are apparent.

The **Hoopoe** *(Upupa epops)* Greek *"Poupouksios"*, is also a very striking bird with its magnificent crest which resembles a fan when raised. It is pale pink in colour with striking black bars across the back and tail. It favours open or wooded countryside and spends much of its time sitting on the ground or in a tree. It likes to make its nest in the hole of an **Olive** or **Carob** tree as well as in the crevice of a cliff or the wall of a building.

A small, predominately black and white bird of telephone wires and pine trees is the **Masked Shrike** *(Lanius nubicus)* Greek *"Thakkanoura"*. It arrives in April in the foothills of the mountains where it lays 3-6 eggs. It can be heard singing constantly while nest-building. It leaves for Africa in September.

From as far away as India, the **Black Headed Bunting** *(Emberiza Melanocephalus)* Greek *"Konthromitis o mavrokefalos"*, arrives to join the other visitors, building nests in small bushes and on vines. The male is very striking in colour, bright yellow and black with a reddish back. He likes perching on tree tops for hours while the female sits on the eggs. The male usually arrives on the island first in April, followed a fortnight later by the female.

A similar species the **Cretzmar's Bunting** *(Emberiza caesia)* *"Konthromitis o eruthrogon"* arrives in Cyprus from Africa in March. It is a small, tubby bird and the male is quite different in colour from the female. The male is brown with a conspicuous blue-grey head, a rust-coloured throat and under parts and a "moustache". The female is striped brown, also with a "moustache". It likes to nest in the foothills of the mountains, laying 3-5 eggs in nests of grass lined with goat hair.

My final choice in this arbitrary selection is the **Roller** *(Coracias garrulus)* Greek *"Karakaksa"* because it is so unique. It can be seen in Cyprus from April until September, usually in the first two months. It is a pale blue bird with a reddish brown back and a heavy

Nightingale

Masked
Shrike

Black Headed
Bunting

Cretzmar's
Bunting

(V)

Pelican

(R)

black crow-like bill. The wings are bright blue with black edges. It does not make nests but likes to lay its eggs in the holes of old buildings.

No other European country can compete with Cyprus in the number of local and migratory birds and different species that can be seen. Unfortunately, their numbers are mostly diminishing each year due to carelessness by the individual.

I hope that this small chapter about our feathered friends will help to make people aware of their beauty, and of the need to preserve and treasure our bird population.

> "The best gun for every hunter is the CONSCIENCE"
> *(Theohari Solea – Reptiles – Snakes)*

Members of the Cyprus Ornithological Society work with much devotion and enthusiasm to promote bird protection on the island. Mr Pavlos Neophytos, the Secretary of the Society keeps records and will supply further information. The address to write to is:— 4 Kanaris Street, Strovolos, Nicosia.

The Cyprus Tourist Office who has branches in every main town also produces a list of the most common birds seen in Cyprus.

For further reading, I would recommend the *"Common Birds of Cyprus"* by J.M.E. Took, published by Kevork K. Keshishian, Nicosia.

SWALLOWS

The swallows slice the evening air
like scimitars in flight
With alternating surfaces
of deepest blue and white;
Their flashing choreography
inspires the human heart
With sheer exhilaration
in their aerobatic art.

Collison-course catastrophes
avoided at the last
Excite a sweet smile of success
as each bird flashes past;
With barrel-roll and loop-the-loop
and high-speed swooping dive
They seem to symbolise the thrill
of simply being alive.

Joie-de-vivre, exuberance,
their freedom of expression
Is purely for their own amusement,
not for vain impression;
Exulting in their flying skills
with house-martins and swifts,
So blessed with talent, fully stretched,
they savour nature's gifts.

A CLOUD OF BUTTERFLIES

The very rich and diversified flora of the island, together with its location, has contributed towards the high butterfly population in Cyprus. Moths are also very prevalent. Sadly, however, the numbers are diminishing each year due to modern farming methods and carelessness resulting, as a consequence, in a decrease in the flora on which butterflies are dependent. It is thought that approximately 80% of all flowering plants are pollinated by insects so that both are dependent on each other.

In Cyprus it has been recorded that 50 different species and sub-species have lived on the island. It is also ideally located between Africa and Europe to act as a resting ground for thousands of migrating butterflies. The islanders refer to these butterflies descending on their land as a **"Cloud of Butterflies"** *(Sinnefo tis petalouthes)*.

The butterflies which flutter past you on the nature trails are so colourful and delicate they are a delight to behold. The following are just a few of my own personal favourites:—

The **Cyprus Meadow Brown** (Maniola cypricola) is one of the butterflies which are endemic to Cyprus. It can be sighted in protected areas almost all the year round, and is most common in chalky areas and stony hillsides. Look for any aromatic plant and you may be fortunate enough to see one. It is dark beige on the underside and has an orange upperpart. On the edge of its wing it has a black spot, resembling an eye. This is nature's way of providing the butterfly with a form of survival for the eye will encourage any predators to attack a harmless area of the body, thus increasing its chance to escape.

Another very attractive butterfly also endemic to Cyprus is the **Paphos Blue** *(Glaucopsyche paphos),* a unique species where the males are a light purple in colour and the females light brown with black spots on the upper parts. This butterfly is on the wing between

February and September and, although, it is most common in Paphos, it can also be sighted in the Troodos foothills. Look for the **Prickly Broom** *(Calycotome villosa),* Greek *Raski,* and the **Paphos Blue** will not be far away.

Another butterfly you may observe on your country walks is the **Speckled Wood** *(Pararge aegaria)* which is most common in forest areas, no higher than 1500m. It is sometimes also sighted in towns. As its name indicates it is brown and orange speckled with tiny eye spots near the edge of the wing. A significant characteristic of this butterfly is that the male defends its own sunny area by chasing off all other males.

Another favourite of mine is the **Swallow Tail** *(Papilio machaon giganteus)* which is on the wing between February and October.

The design on the upperpart of this butterfly together with the shape of the wings strongly remind you of the bird, the **Swallow Tail,** hence its name. The speckled colouring is brown, yellow and navy blue. It may be sighted in any area in Cyprus where the Umbelliferae family of plants grow e.g. **Fennel** Greek *Anarthrika.* A characteristic of this butterfly is that its caterpillar has a natural defence mechanism against predators. It has a reddish organ behind its head from which ejects a foul smell.

If you are lucky, you may spot my final choice, the **Red Admiral** *(Vanessa atlanta)* along the nature trail. Although not common in Cyprus it can be sighted in grassy areas, perhaps river valleys, in cool locations any time from Spring until late December. Its predominant colours are brownish-black and orange with splashes of white on the forewings and some dots of black on the hind wings. There is also a fine tracing of blue along the outer edge of the forewings and a touch of blue at the angle of the hind wings.

In conclusion one must always remember that for us to enjoy these butterflies as nature intended, we must preserve our flora and protect the countryside, or too many of them may become extinct.

For further reading: *"Nature of Cyprus"* by C. Georgiades;

"Butterflies of Cyprus" by R. Parker,
Entomologist Gazette, Vol. 34, March 1983;

"Butterflies of Britain and Europe" by
L.G. Higgins and N.D. Riley, Collins.

(V)

(J)

ΚΥΠΡΟΣ-KIBRIS-CYPRUS ΚΥΠΡΟΣ-KIBRIS-CYPRUS ΚΥΠΡΟΣ-KIBRIS-CYPRU

Butterflies on Cyprus Stamps.

(V)

THE BUTTERFLY

Polychromatic sunshine spills
onto each powdered wing,
As light-as-light, they wander
through the many blossomed spring;
The dowdy flowers glower
as they gaily flutter by,
For who could match the colours
of the Cyprus butterfly.

REPTILES

The wide open surf-swept beach at Lara in the Akamas peninsular has become the breeding ground for two forms of **Turtle,** the **Loggerhead Turtle** *(Caretta caretta)* and the **Green Turtle** *(Chelonia mydas).* These once endangered species have been saved from extinction by the Department of Fisheries and the Ministry of Agriculture and Natural Resources, who set up a conservation project in 1978.

Visitors are not unwelcome to Lara and the Turtle project. The way is sign-posted from Ayios Yeorgios, but the track is long and difficult. The area is protected from an overflow of tourism in order that the breeding can survive.

Lizards are very common on the island, my own particular favourite being the **Mediterranean Chameleon** *(Chamaeleo chameleon),* a small reptile whose colour changes according to its background. It is found in gardens, cultivated areas and bushy areas where it searches for food. It feeds mainly on insects which it catches with its long tongue. It inflates its body when in danger but the **Chameleon** itself is harmless.

Seven kinds of snakes now exist in Cyprus. Formerly, there were eleven different kinds, the last one being the **Grass Snake** in 1960.

The most common snake to be found on the island is the **Large Whip Snake** *(Coluber jugalaris).* It is a very large, slim snake which can reach 3 metres in length. For the first three years of its life, this snake is yellowish-brown in colour and then it becomes black. It eats rats, mice, birds and lizards, and is harmless to humans. The **Large Whip Snake** can be seen all over Cyprus. It is the only snake in Cyprus that does not need a special habitat to live there.

A relatively rare snake, but one which is endemic to Cyprus, is the **Cyprus Whip Snake** *(Coluber cypriensis)* whose base colour on the upper side is olive-brown. It prefers to live in the hills and mountains rather than along the coast. This snake is also harmless to humans.

(R)

(R)

(R)

The other two harmless snakes which are to be found in Cyprus is the very small **Worm Snake** *(Typhlos vermicularis)* and the strong **Coin Snake** *(Coluber nummifer)*. The remaining three are poisonous snakes although not one of the snakes in Cyprus will attack humans voluntarily.

The **Blunt-nosed Viper** *(Vipera lebetina)* is the most venomous. It is a big viper with a sturdy head, clearly distinguishable from the neck. In colour it is whitish-grey, straw-yellow to rust-brown. It likes to live in quiet areas, preferably dry river beds with small pools where it waits for prey such as birds, rats, mice and sometimes other snakes too. In defence this snake will bite with a very strong poison which must be treated by an antidote. It is interesting in that only the **Blunt-nosed Viper** bears a live baby snake whereas all the other snakes in Cyprus lay eggs.

The other two poisonous snakes are:— the **Montpellier Snake** *(Malpolon monspessulanus)* which is a remarkably fast and agile snake, fleeing at the slightest danger whilst uttering a strong hiss. It is not dangerous to man normally because it moves so quickly; and finally the rather rare and slim **Cat Snake** *(Telescopus fallax)* which is also harmless to humans because its small head and mouth do not allow its poisonous fangs to penetrate.

An expert on snakes here in Cyprus is Mr. George Wiedl Hans-Jorg who will be happy to provide you with any further information you may require. His address is P.O. Box 2133, Paphos.

Any further details regarding turtles may be obtained from the Department of Fisheries and the Ministry of Agriculture and Natural Resources in Nicosia.

(H)

(M)

(H)

(H)

(H)

MAMMALS

All over the Cyprus landscape tinkling bells can be heard indicating that a flock of sheep or goats, sometimes together, are not too far away. Always accompanied by a shepherd and a dog the animals are kept under excellent control. This is important because otherwise, left to their own devices, they would simply strip the land bare of plant life and valuable vegetables.

Most **sheep** and **goats** are very nimble-footed so you may often encounter them both in the lowlands and the mountains. The shepherds who tend them look hardened and agile too, perhaps from the exercise and fresh air but undoubtedly from drinking the animals' milk. **Goat's** milk is sold throughout the island — it is highly nutritious and free from the *tubercle baccilus*. From the milk the locals produce the famous Cyprus cheese called "Halloumi". Try it grilled — it is delicious!

If you find it difficult to distinguish the difference between the Cyprus goat and sheep, look at their horns.

The **goat's** horns are flat and swept back while the sheep's horns curve downwards and forwards.

Sheep have woolly coats whereas **goats** are hairy except that some breeds produce a kind of wool called mohair. Both male and female **goats** have beards known as "tassels". **Goats** tend to be more energetic and active than their timid companions. Both animals originated in Asia and sheep originated from the European **Moufflon.**

About 1500-2000 extremely rare **Cyprus Moufflon,** locally *Agrina,* exist in a special reserve in the Paphos Forest at Stavros tis Psokas. These beautiful, wild mountain sheep were hunted nearly to extinction earlier this century. In 1938 only 15-20 animals had survived, and the Government declared the **Moufflon** as an endangered species and immediately set up a programme for their conservation.

(R)

The male **Moufflon** is a very sturdy and proud animal, timid and swift in its movement. The horns are curved like ordinary sheep. Their summer coat for both males and females is short, pale brown in colour with white underparts. The winter coat is thick brown hair with light grey across the shoulder blades. It is usually spotted in the early morning or late afternoon.

From the inspection of fossilised bones of Ancient mammals, it would seem that the fauna of former times were quite different from the fauna seen on Cyprus today. Animals such as the **Pigmy Elephant,** the **Pigmy Hippopotamus, Wild Boar** and **Grecian Ibex** all were prevalent during that time. Only the Cyprus **Moufflon** has survived.

The ubiquitous **donkey** is still a cherished beast of burden here on the island. Other mammals which can be encountered include the **Cyprian Hare,** the **Cyprian Shrew,** the **Cyprian Spring Mouse,** the **Rat,** the **Eared Hedgehog,** the **Fox** and various species of **bats.**

For more information see *'Nature of Cyprus'* by C. Georgiades.

(R)

(M)

(R)

EPILOGUE

With regard to collecting and preserving wild flowers, please be discerning and exercise restraint. The feet of a keen naturalist can do as much damage to the plants as a tourist who walks over them without seeing them. It is essential for the heritage of Cyprus to preserve its flora.

NATURE'S TREASURE

These fragile flowers are Nature's treasure
Provided not just for our pleasure
For they exist without mankind;
We must preserve them where we find
Them struggling to survive, for we
In trust control their destiny.
Their sights we see, their scents we breathe;
As we inherit, so we bequeathe.

I hope this book will act as an inspiration to those fortunate enough to live in Cyprus — to look, learn and appreciate the natural beauty this island has to offer. Too many of us take this for granted.

For visitors I trust you will find the guide useful during your explorations, and act as a pleasant reminder of a truly unique and colourful landscape; the natural charm that is Cyprus.

APPENDIX

For further interest, I append some information below about th
herbalists whose names I quote on previous pages:—

Hippocrates (born 460BC), the famous Greek doctor, wrote book
emphasising the importance of diet and hygiene
His scientific writings and practical work ridicule
the supernatural aspect of primitive medicine. Hi
books included about 400 simple remedies.

Theophrastus (born 370BC) wrote *"Enquiry into Plants",* a study o
the structure of plants and was the first to classif
plants.

Pliny the Elder (AD 23-79) a Roman Civil Servant, wrote *"Natura
History"* which he dedicated to the Emperor Titus
His scientific observations were heavily laced with
superstition but the volume of his work has made i
a valuable source of reference for herbal writers
Pliny died of fumes and exhaustion while investi
gating the eruption of Vesuvius.

Dioscorides, Pedanius (1st C AD) was a Greek physician living in
Rome. In his treatise *"De Materia Medica"* he deal
with the properties of 600 herbs. It was the leading
text on pharmacology for 16 centuries. A copy o
the manuscript was illustrated in about AD 61:
with naturalist watercolours.

Galen, Claudius (AD 30) practised medicine in Rome where he attende
the Emperors M. Aurelius and L. Verus. Next t
Hippocrates he was one of the most famous o
ancient physicians. He wrote a number of books or
medicine.

BIBLIOGRAPHY

.ora of Cyprus (2 vols.) by R.D. Meikle, Kew.

ature of Cyprus, Environment, Flora, Fauna by C. Georgiades, Nicosia.

rchids of Greece and Cyprus by G. Hermjacob, Athens.

ants of Medicine (2 vols.) by C. Georgiades, Nicosia.

he Herb and Spice Book by Sarah Garland, London.

he Green Guide to Health from Plants by Jean Palaiseul, London.

owers of the Mediterranean by Oleg Pulunin and Anthony Huxley, London.

Taste of Cyprus by Gilli Davies, London.

xploring Cyprus by Renos Lavithis, London.

ommon Birds of Cyprus by Y. Took, Nicosia.

Reference to Photographs

(V) — Valerie Sinclair

(R) — Renos Lavithis

(J) — John Taylor

(M) — Mary Guth

(Y) — Yiannis Christofides

(P) — Apostolos Potamos

(M) — Ministry of Agriculture, Department of Forestry.

(H) — George Wiedl Hans-Jorg

(S) — Stephanos Theodorou

(CTO) — Cyprus Tourism Organisation.

INDEX OF ENGLISH NAMES

INDEX OF LATIN NAMES

INDEX OF GREEK NAMES